THE REAL MYSTERY OF
TOM THOMSON

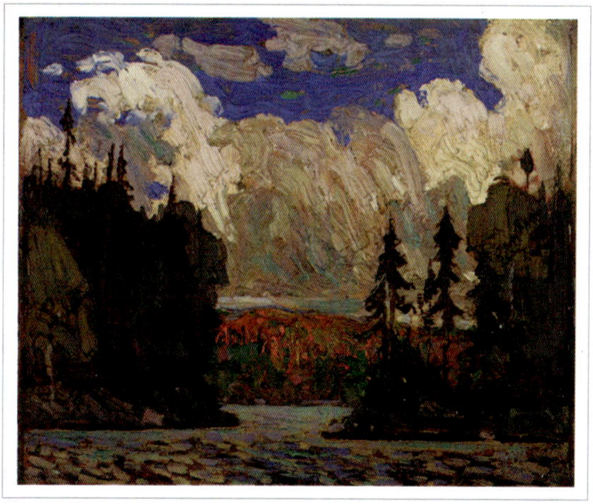

His Art and His Life

Richard Weiser

DRAGON
HILL

The Publisher: Dragon Hill Publishing Ltd.

Library and Archives Canada Cataloguing in Publication
Title: The real mystery of Tom Thomson : his art and his life /
Richard Weiser.
Names: Weiser, Richard, 1967– author.

Description: Includes bibliographical references.
Identifiers: Canadiana (print) 20190106093 | Canadiana (ebook) 20190106115 | ISBN 9781896124742
(softcover) | ISBN 9781896124759 (EPUB)
Subjects: LCSH: Thomson, Tom, 1877-1917. | LCSH: Painters—Canada—Biography.
Classification: LCC ND249.T5 W45 2019 | DDC 759.11—dc23

Project Director: Marina Michaelides
Cover Image: Painting: Tom Thomson, *The Jack Pine,* National Gallery of Canada (1519)
Image Credits: Every effort has been made to accurately credit the sources of the images used in this book. Any errors or omissions should be directed to the publisher for changes in future editions.

Images courtesy of: Allen County Public Library Genealogy Center (p. 57); Archives of Ontario (p. 19, S1927); Art Gallery of Ontario (); Canadian War Museum (p. 107); Edward P. Taylor Research Library and Archives, Art Gallery of Ontario (p. 65, file 19); GettyImages-1051111466.jpg, Photo: paladin13 (pp. 63, 87, 106, 108, 109, 124, 130); 1059857730.jpg, Photo: phokin (pp. 76, 79, 81, 88, 90, 94, 98, 104, 114, 116, 127); 920344872.eps, Photo: AndrewScherbackov (p.106); McMichael Canadian Art Collection (p.1, 1966.14; p. 51; p. 66; p. 76, 1977.31; p.83, 1966.16.76; p. 88, 1966.16.72; p.91, 1966.15.18; p. 113, 1981.9.2); Montreal Museum of Fine Arts (p. 103, 1922.179); National Gallery of Canada (p. 84, no. 16783; p. 95, no. 16779; p. 102, no. 16780; p. 105, no. 16773; p. 118, 1519; p. 125, 4677r); Tom Thomson Art Gallery (p. 30, 988.011.002;); Tom Thomson Art Gallery Permanent Collection (p. 49); The Thomson Collection at the Art Gallery of Ontario, (p. 63, 72/25; p. 75, AGOID.69252; p. 82, 82/176; p.111, L69.49; p. 115, AGOID.69179; p. 120, 784); Trent University Archives, Blowden Davies fonds, Photographer Unknown (p. 16).

Produced with the assistance of the Government of Alberta. Alberta Government

PC: 38

Contents

Dedication

With love, to Erin and our story-loving girls.

Acknowledgements

This book is a 20-year on-again, off-again odyssey, so I have lots of thanks to give. Thanks Erin, Chris Tait and John Cockshutt for your edits and encouragement for the early drafts. Thanks to Trista Vincent and the writers' group–especially David Gamble–for your feedback and friendship. Thanks to Olive Senior and the Humber School for Writers. Thanks to Sarah Davies, Mark Dillon, Hilary McMahon, Arlene MacDougal, Mike O'Connor, Amy Lavender Brown, and Chris Eaton for the introductions. Thanks to Karen Pinchin for your guidance, and for believing in me and this project. And, thanks to Marina Michaelides at Dragon Hill Publishing for making this book a reality.

This project would never have seen the light of day if not for my generous and patient wife, Erin, who told me to take a break from my advertising career and brought home the bacon while I wrote this book.

PROLOGUE

Canoe Lake
Ontario, August 1917

"A plaid overcoat, caps, a worn-out suit, red Hudson Bay blankets, 4 pairs of socks, 2 plates and cups, handkerchiefs, an aluminum pail, an ink bottle, a brown canvas bag, drawers[1], this is about all. Yes, I think this is everything."

Dark brown wax paper enveloped Tom's belongings inside a beach-brown pine crate. The lid was nailed into place, iron biting easily into the obliging wood. Red-haired and sweating freely in his black wool suit, Shannon Fraser slid his hammer along the porch, tiddlywinking scales of paint from the chapped boards. He harvested sweat from his forehead with a shiny sleeve and donned his misshapen black felt hat.

"Ho man! Chubby, gimmie a hand here!"

Fraser's assistant, George Chubb, rangy and unshaven, loped in from the beach to help shift the crate. The midday heat flattened trees, cottages, and immobilized the lake, while treetops were tousled by the shrilling of cicadas. Horses clip-clopped dully along a tree-shaded dirt lane roadway to Canoe Lake Station, their smooth backs dappled by transient islands of light.

Two hundred miles to the south, in the Gallery of Art at Toronto's Canadian National Exhibition, nested amongst pastoral landscapes and portraits of dogs: a twisted pine bent like a lyre; a robin's egg blue sky contending with piebald clouds; a whitecapped lake; distant hillocks loitering grey and green; the smell of sun on fallen pine needles; the sound of wind in the trees.

A New Picture of Tom Thomson

I discovered Tom Thomson in the fall of 1980. Canadian pride was high in Pierre Trudeau's Canada, and I was receptive to the "Notable Canadians" section of grade six social studies. The intrepid painter loomed large amongst luminaries such as Laura Secord, record-breaking athlete Tom Longboat and heroic Doctor Norman Bethune.

What really hooked me on Thomson was that he was a canoeist, and he had lived in and painted Algonquin Park. My great-grandfather had built a cottage on nearby Lake of Bays, and I was a decent canoeist myself, having mastered the elusive J-stroke the previous summer. I loved the rocky terrain, the sandy lakes, the jagged pines and bone-white birches. For me it was a refuge from the monotony of the suburbs and the social challenges of public school.

It was a dissonance; however, that the landscapes he painted were inhospitable and sinister.

The most influential analysis of Thomson's paintings comes from cultural theorist Northrup Frye who, in the 1940s, wrote:

> *What is essential in Thomson is the imaginative instability, the emotional unrest and dissatisfaction one feels about a country which has not been lived in: the tension between the mind and a surrounding not integrated with it.*[2]

In several pictures one has the feeling of something not quite emerging, which is all the more sinister for its concealment.[3]

Frye called this sinister something The Canadian sphinx.

When the Canadian sphinx brought her riddle of unvisualized land to Thomson it did not occur to him to hide under the bedclothes, though she did not promise him money, fame, happiness or even self-confidence, and when she was through with him, she scattered his bones in the wilderness.[4]

According to Frye, because the land in Thomson's paintings is unlived in, unvisualized, the mind—of Thomson and the viewers of the painting—cannot contemplate it without "turning it into the monstrous,"[5] hence the sphinx. I love this idea of a sphinx, with a riddle to be solved. And in my studies of Thomson and his work, I happened across a mystery of my own: If Thomson's paintings are not sinister depictions of an inhospitable land, what are they? What does the Canadian sphinx have to reveal to us?

When I first encountered it, Frye's interpretation seemed flawed. I knew the country Thomson painted, and it was hardly the far north.[6] It is cottage country and has been since been since my great-grandfather built his cottage in 1902. Cottages dotted the landscape on many of the lakes in Algonquin Park, as well as hotels, even a children's summer camp.[7] Large-scale lumber operations punctuated countryside, and a railway cut across the park. While forests dominated, and farms and cities were absent, Algonquin Park was most certainly lived in.

Is it possible that despite the Park Rangers, tourists and cottagers, Thomson felt the land was inhospitable, even monstrous? Is that what we see in his landscapes? At 13, my attentions soon wandered to post-punk music, Dungeons and Dragons, and girls with Dorothy Hamill bobs and dancing eyes, but somewhere in my mind the dissonance remained.

Fast-forward to the winter of 2014 in Toronto. Now a happily married, middle-aged father of two living in west-end Toronto, I had taken a year off my work as an advertising copywriter to write a book about Tom Thomson. It started off as a straightforward biography but in a style meant to capture the gorgeous colours and staccato poetry of his sketches. As I wrote, it became something else. That dissonance I felt in my childhood began to reassert itself when I wrote about Thomson's cousin, William Brodie, who was the director of the Biology Department at the Provincial Museum in the early 20th century.

Brodie was an amateur naturalist who became a key member of the scientific community in Toronto. He embraced Darwin's theory of evolution[8] at a time when many believed God had ordained mankind to have dominion over "every living thing that moveth upon the earth."[9] In a literal as well as spiritual sense[10], he believed than humans were "a part of nature, not apart from nature."[11]

Maybe during the many walks and talks they had together,[12] Brodie told Thomson that humans, that Thomson himself, was an integral part of the natural world. Maybe when Thomson painted those wild pictures, he was showing us the vibrant, vital landscape in which we belonged, as opposed to an inhospitable, sinister world in which we have no place. Could this be the answer to the mystery of the Canadian sphinx?

Finally, I found a crucial clue in the archives, deep in the bowels of the Royal Ontario Museum. In a non-descript cardboard box, amongst yellowed letters and sepia photographs, was the private journal of William Brodie.

–Richard Weiser
January 2016

CHAPTER ONE

The Pointers
The Thomson Family in Canada

Tom Thomson emigrated to Canada from Scotland in 1832. Not the painter, but his grandfather of the same name. This first Thomson left the lairds and tenanted fields of St. Fergus for the dream of his own land in Upper Canada.

This was a time before steam-powered ocean liners, so Thomson sailed on a three-masted *coffin ship* that brought a steady flow of British Isles emigrants to the New World.

***Picture this:** Thomson descends 'tween deck into the steerage stink and daylight darkness of a trans-Atlantic voyage, where moans of the ill and weeping of the grief-stricken rob him of sleep. The overboard splash of bodies cause an involuntary shiver: yet another burial at sea.*[13]

After six harrowing weeks, Thomson emerged from the ship's depths but only into the purgatory of a quarantine shack in Grosse Île below Quebec.[14] All around him, cholera raged through Lower Canada. After what must have seemed a lifetime, he was released and took a ferry to the river's head, with a thousand islands and a lake as large as a sea.

In 1837, rebellion swirled through the Canadas. Lieutenant-Governor Francis Bond Head maintained the status quo through a campaign of violence and fraud. With his fiery rhetoric, "rebel-rouser" William Lyon Mackenzie convinced farmers and city folk alike that revolution was the only way to wrest power from the Family Compact, the ruling elite. The result? A historical fizzle, and the only mutual retreat in Canadian history.

While Bond Head raged and Mackenzie ran, Thomson settled in Pickering Township. He bought 20 hectares of prime farmland near Nobel's corner store, less than a day's ride from the city of York—the seat of his majesty's representative in Upper Canada. A dream realized after years of labour on other farmer's lands, half a world away from where he started.

Thomson had been courting Betty Brodie, lately arrived from St. Fergus with her family in tow: Aunt Jean, Uncle George and their five children including William, who would become a dentist, an amateur botanist and a mentor to Canada's greatest painter. Thomson and Betty were married in 1839. Together they worked the land. Their first year was a difficult one: a cow lost to the woods; dogs gone feral killed their sheep. And then Betty took ill, but still she helped log and clear, spending many a day "binding grain behind the cradlers."[15] With luck and labour they persevered, and though he "never filled a six-penny's worth of paper in school,"[16] Thomson wrote himself onto the land.

Together the Thomsons raised their son, John, sending him to school in nearby Whitby. Thomson took him hunting and fishing. John learned how to trace his name over his father's fields, a palimpsest.

Margaret Matheson's people traded the red earth of PEI for brown. Her father Kenneth, a builder of homes, could not keep his household whole. After his wife died, he sent his daughter off to be a servant in the Thomson home. It was there John and Margaret met and fell in love.[17]

With his education, John could have had a career in business, but instead he chose the land over neckties and ledgers.[18] When he and Margaret married in 1865, the first Tom Thomson and Betty retired to the stone cottage they had built nearby.[19]

In 1867, Canada was confederated amid promises of railways, and soon the first of the next generation of Thomsons was born, starting with George. He was followed by Elizabeth, Henry, Louise, and Mary, their names reproducing the British royals.

In the summer of 1874, Betty died followed by Thomson the subsequent spring. No longer immigrants, they became a part of the land they had worked.

In 1877, two years after his grandfather died, Tom Thomson, his namesake, was born. Written into being with his forefather's names. It is a circular name: Tom's son John's son, Tom John Thomson. Tom, from the Greek, ultimately Aramaic, *te'oma,* meaning, "twin." The name was originally an epithet for Jesus's disciple *Yehuda,* the second Jude: Doubting Thomas. An apt name for a man for whom self-confidence would never come easy.

Tom was only a baby when the family moved to Rosehill, an elegant farmhouse a few fields from Georgian Bay in the

Hamlet of Leith, near Owen Sound. The terrain was flat, tree-covered, hunching inland into hills. John was so excited to make the purchase after such a long search, he left six thousand dollars unattended in his democrat wagon while he was in the lawyer's office making final arrangements.[20]

Tom Thomson and the Land

So what is Thomson's relationship with the land? His forbearers, his namesakes, are farmers. His grandfather, who he would have heard about in stories, left his home in Scotland and laboured for years to establish his farm in Claremont. His father, John, made a conscious choice to pursue farming. With his education he could have gone into business, perhaps become a dentist as his mother's cousin, William Brodie, had done. But John chose the farm.

This is the world into which Tom Thomson was born. He was brought up on a farm, worked on a farm and went to school with the children of farmers.

The relationship between the farmer and the land is unique. They literally live off the land, shape it to their needs and depend on it for their livelihood. Raised in these circumstances, Thomson would have understood, intimately, the reciprocity between the farmer and the farm. The person and the land. The land of Thomson's formative years was Leith, Ontario.

CHAPTER TWO

Early Spring, Tom's Childhood in Leith

At Rosehill John began afresh, filling fields with flowers and herbs instead of cash crops,[21] certainly not the custom for a working farm. Leith native Alan Ross described John Thomson as a "rather a unique character at Leith. He was a gentleman in every sense but one of the most eccentric men who ever drew the breath of life."[22]

In Leith, the Thomson household grew to include Margaret's sister Henrietta and their niece, Charlotte "Lottie" Tripp, daughter of their deceased sister, Catherine. All of the girls were called by diminutives: Minnie, Lizzie, Lottie. Four more children were born to John and Margaret here, siblings for Tom: Margaret "Peggy," Ralph, James and Fraser. The latter named after the pastor of nearby Leith Presbyterian Church.[23]

When Tom was five, his brother James died—a baby, merely nine months old. It was an early brush with death. I imagine Tom wondered why the earth "…took him to itself?" The very words painter, and future mentor to Tom, J.E.H. MacDonald would eventually write for Tom's own cairn. James shared a plot with Tom's maternal grandfather, the homebuilder, Kenneth Matheson, the same plot Tom himself now shares, or at least, the tombstone that bears his name.

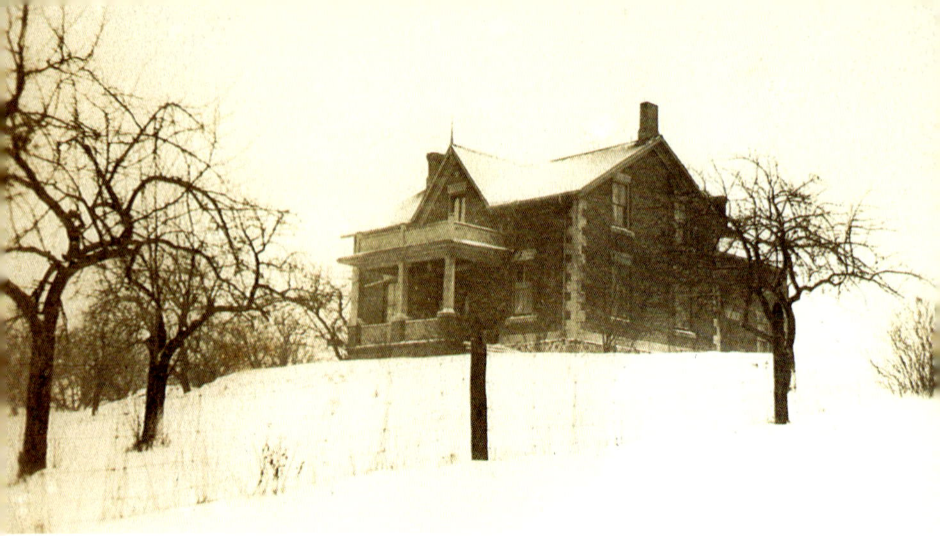

Rosehill, the Thomson Family Farmhouse, Leith, Ontario, Blodwen Davies fonds. Photographer unknown. Courtesy of Trent University Archives

About this same time in Toronto, William Brodie—dentist, amateur botanist, cousin to Tom's grandmother—was mourning the loss of his only son, "Sweet William." He drowned when his canoe overturned on the Assiniboine River. A boy-shaped hole opened in Brodie's life that would only be filled when Tom settled in Toronto in the next century.

On the Thomson farm, "each member of the family shouldered a share of the responsibility and work. In that way there was always leisure for the finer things of life, such as music, literature and hospitality"[24] and, of course, art. All of the Thomson children were fond of drawing.[25] They drew at home, at school[26], even at church.[27] Tom loved to draw the ships he saw on the bay, their sails set to breeze.[28] Tom's sister Minnie recalled,

> *Sometimes Tom would take a notion to draw such funny caricatures of people we knew. He would keep us all laughing and guessing who they were. Always while he drew he whistled and sang and I can still see the whimsical grin he wore when he got a particularly good caricature.*[29]

John was later at a loss to account, by any law of heredity, how artists should be among his offspring.

At night the family sang around the piano; they read.

***Picture this:** Tom's head warm against his mother's chest, he hears Byron, Dickens, Burns, Scott, reverberate through her body as Auntie Henrietta strokes his straight brown hair.*

Tom's father read to them also. Tom's sister, Louise, recalled:

> *He was reading the death of little Paul in* [Dickens'] *Dombey and Son, and he was so overcome with the pathos of it that he had us all in tears and he could not finish. He said, "Oh I can't read it, you'll just have to read it for yourselves and he walked out."*[30]
>
> *I remember one night Father wakened the whole household laughing at Dickens' description of an American eating horse at breakfast. Mother asked him what he was laughing at and he got the book and tried to read the passage to us but was overcome again at the humour of it.*[31]

In 1885, the country's focus turned west. The railway connecting the country east to west was finally finished. The North-West Rebellion ended with the capture of rebel leader Louis Riel at the Battle of Batoche by General Frederick Middleton.

While the last spike was struck and poor Riel hanged, Tom went to school with his siblings. An indifferent student, Tom was, "clever enough at his studies but he lacked the faculty of concentration,"[32] not like his brother Ralph.[33] Outside the school, horseshoes ca-chink on the road, the murmur of voices, the thrum of the wind. Tom's mother helped the children with history and literature, his father with mathematics and grammar.[34]

Tom played with the village boys, the Rosses and McKeens: "swings, skipping ropes, sleds, lawn croquet, a merry go round."[35] His sister Louise remembered:

> *He was very fond of sports and was an ardent football player before he left home, and in one game he had one great toe broken but stayed with the game till the finish, kicking with the left foot. Of all outdoor sports, I believe fishing was his favourite pastime.*[36]

Minnie also recalled Tom's love of fishing, "I can see him first as a small boy with a string of fish caught in the creek where he would clean and smoke in a piece of stove pipe, and I still remember how delicious they were."[37]

Tom's father and grandfather were also avid fishermen.[38] John taught his son to make his own lures based on the insects the fish were eating at that specific time.[39] He would have told Tom that this was simply the right way to fish. This was John's way. "With him right was right and wrong was wrong, there could be no compromise."[40] Tom's father mirrored an absolute sense of self for Tom: you were either right or wrong; good or bad; total success or an absolute failure.

On one occasion, Tom's sister Minnie noticed a girl at school copying her schoolwork. She told her father and he replied, "As I see it, she is committing a crime. And you are an accomplice".[41] From John, Tom learned to prize sincerity, to hold snobbery and hypocrisy in contempt.[42]

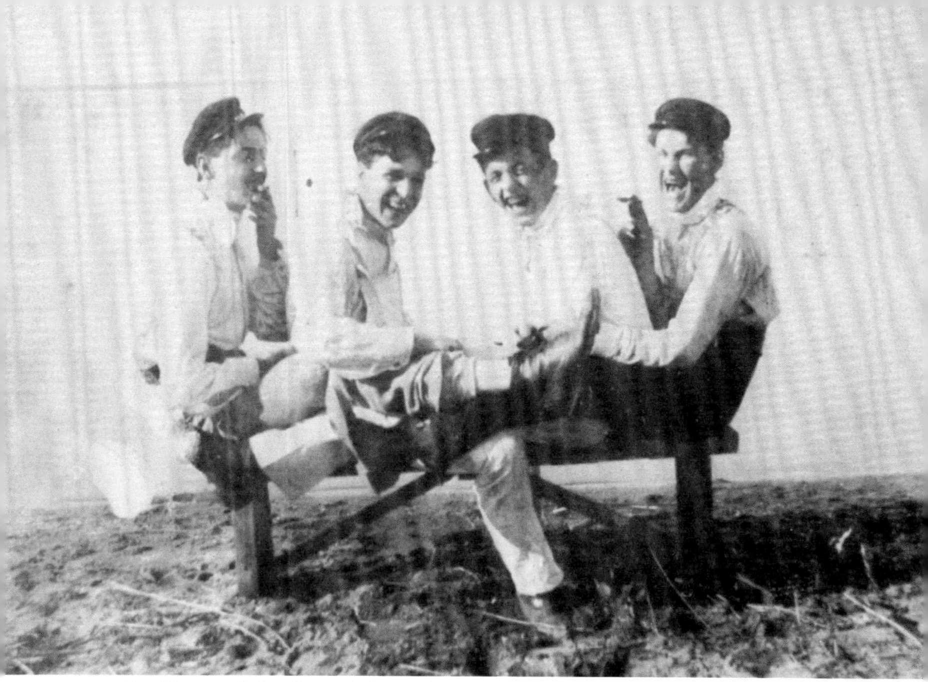

Tom Thomson (left) and Friends, [ca. 1908], Archives of Ontario

At first, Tom shared a room with George, eight years his elder: George the scholar, George the musician, George with his dashing moustache. When Tom was twelve, George left home for business school. John's firstborn chose neckties and ledgers over the land.

Tom took George's place in the village band. He attempted the tenor trombone, then the cornet. "At the best, however, he was never the musician such as his three brothers, George, Henry and Ralph, became. Henry...played cornet, violin and piano and played them all superlatively well."[43] In time Tom mastered the humble mandolin,[44] practicing for hours until the tips of his fingers were scalloped and red.

Tom and the band played local dances, "Green Grow the Rashes," "Banks and Braes of Bonnie Doon." "They played rather intoxicating dance music and with a flawless maple floor in the hall, a good time was a foregone conclusion."[45] Although Tom would have been uncomfortable being the center of attention, the stage creates a space, a distance that allows one to perform unselfconsciously. I imagine he turned his face to the ground when the crowd applauded.

Tom grew quite fond of a girl from school, a girl who sang in the choir. After she read out a letter from Tom to her friends, he found out and declared, "That's the end of it."[46] On another occasion he worked up the courage to ask a different girl to the dance. They met, danced and parted, all without more than a few words from Tom.[47] Although he was a fine singer and dancer, and enjoyed both, he would never be popular with the ladies, who found him distant, reticent, strange.

Tom loved to be on the water. He fished, swam and rowed the family rowboat, but ever since he drew sketches of sailboats on Owen Sound, he really wanted to sail.[48] Louise Thomson recounts:

> *He had pleaded with Father for permission to put a small sail on the family row boat and Father finally consented. When Tom and his chum David Ross had the boat ready for the try out, there was a stiff breeze blowing and as luck would have it, Joe Coture, French Canadian fisherman and an expert sailor came in sight with his two masted fishing boat, which had the reputation of being the fastest boat of its kind on the lake, under the able management of Old Joe, as he was familiarly called by the younger generation. In telling of the big outing afterwards David said, "We passed old Joe so fast, we made him think he was backing up."*[49]

Like other Canadian boys of their age, I imagine they played at being Captain Cook fighting at doomed Wolfe's side. Tom might have played at being Étienne Brûlé, leading Indian raids on the shores of La Mer Douce, but his father wouldn't let him canoe.[50] Too dangerous.

One October, Tom and Dave's brother, Alan, were trolling for lake trout in the sail/rowboat when a sudden storm rolled in.

> *About 50 yards from shore, at the time of the first event, our boat swung into the trough and over we went, lines, oars, lunch basket, fish, fishing tackle—everything—all rolled up on the beach on the big combers that were sweeping in, while we were wading to dry footing up to our waists in water. My brother Dave and two others were there waiting for us and they received us as though we were returned from the dead. We had pulled for about 4 miles through one of the worst blows I ever saw on Georgian Bay, in an 18-foot skiff, and I noticed at the time that Tom, who was rowing in the bow, never once spoke. He never would speak about such things, even afterwards.*[51]

When Tom was 17, he wanted to leave the farm, leave Leith, sail the Great Lakes. But his mother, Margaret, feared for his health, and his father John would have missed the (free) labour on the farm. Instead, Tom stayed with his younger brothers, Ralph and Fraser, and sister Margaret until he came of age, until he came into his inheritance from his grandfather's, his namesake's, estate.[52]

During Wednesday evening admonitions at Leith Presbyterian, Dr. Fraser frowned his congregation into grace. There, Tom's downturned face turned red as he and his friends were dressed down for wearing their work clothes to church.[53] From the Gospel of St. Matthew:

> *And when the king came in to see the guests, he saw there a man who had not on a wedding garment. And he*

was speechless. Then said the king unto the servants, bind him hand and foot, and take him away, and cast him into the outer darkness; there shall be weeping and gnashing of teeth. For many are called, but few are chosen.[54]

Tom Thomson Searches for his Place

Tom Thomson was born and raised on a farm, the descendant and namesake of farmers. He heard the stories of his grandfather's sacrifices to gain his own land, of how his father chose the land over a career in business, despite his education. On this farm, he learned about the reciprocal relationship between farmer and farm, between the person and the land.

It is important to note, in the face of the bucolic mythology that has grown up around him, that Thomson was not raised on a farm in the wilderness. He grew up just outside the bustling port city of Owen Sound. Grain from the prairies was unloaded from Great Lakers while goods from all points in Ontario, Quebec, New England and overseas were unloaded from boxcars into the emptied freighters.

This was absolutely not an "unlived-in" land guarded by a sinister sphinx. The land had been cleared and farmed for decades.[55] It was located right next to a major port city. While Thomson's brush with drowning would have given him some respect for the power of nature, it certainly didn't scare him off boating or swimming as evidenced by his love of both throughout his life.[56]

Obviously, Thomson left Leith and the farm, becoming a painter...eventually. But it would be a long time before he visited Algonquin Park, and his painting career began.

Thomson's inclination to see things as either entirely good or bad, complete success or absolute failure, made his journey to artistic competence a painful one. To make things even more difficult, this black-and-white thinking extended to his personal relationships as well.

> *I think that with the exception of his brother Ralph, of Seattle, Wash*[ington], *he was the most generous and open-hearted man it has ever been my fortune to know. However, he had strange antipathies, and the few people he did dislike he hated most cordially; he was not at all diplomatic in concealing it either.*[57]

As children we get our sense of self from our parents. It is mirrored back to us and becomes the self we see. As adults we seek identity through social membership and employment. With his "strange antipathies," Thomson did not find his place in the world easily. Indeed, I believe that the difficulty in belonging that he experienced in his adulthood contributed to the importance of belonging once, and where, he finally found it. And, although Thomson did indeed leave the land, leave the farm, he eventually re-established a relationship very much in line with that of his namesake farming forefathers, although in a different way, and only after a long, and often painful, search for a place he belonged.

CHAPTER THREE

Morning Cloud
Tom Leaves Home

At twenty-one Tom inherited a $2000.00 legacy from his grandfather, its expenditure evidenced by its absence later on.[58] Some of the money went to membership fees for the Ancient Order of Foresters[59]—Dr. Oronhyatekha, the Supreme Chief Ranger and CEO—an organization dedicated to helping those who "fell into need walking through the forests of life." It provided sick pay, funeral grants and a measure of independence and peace of mind for Tom.

Some of the legacy went towards an apprenticeship at William Kennedy and Sons machine shop and foundry in Owen Sound[60] where Tom's friend, Alan Ross, was already employed as a machinist.

> *I had started an apprenticeship in the machinist's trade with the Wm. Kennedy and Sons at Owen Sound in 1894. Tom apprenticed himself with the same firm in the winter of 1899. He only lasted about eight months at this, however. He and the foreman, a gentleman named Munro, never got along, and in August of that year Tom quit.*

> *He told me about 3 years later that it was the most regrettable incident in his life until then and that he often thought of going back at the trade.*[61]

Tom visited the taverns of Owen Sound and occasionally bought a bottle. Some nights, "there was absolutely no sense to the manner in which Tom set about his drinking when the humour seemed to take him."[62] Alan Ross wrote:

> *I have been with him on several occasions when I am now sorry to say that neither of us was very sober, but it is in such times men exchange real confidences and it was on one such occasion that I discovered how deeply sensitive he was and how he resented anything like public ridicule.*[63]
>
> *I remember one night in 1901, in Meaford, when he unbosomed himself, lamenting his lack of success in life in terms that rather astonished me. I began to think then that he realized his powers and that he also had secret ambitions.*[64]

After the failed apprenticeship at the foundry, Tom spent more of his inheritance on tuition for the Canadian Business College in Chatham, Ontario, "Canada's Greatest School of Business," pursuing neckties and ledgers. This was the same school Tom's brother Henry had attended, and also his eldest brother George, who had been on the honour roll. Tom studied bookkeeping, banking and penmanship. Concentration would have been an issue for Tom.[65] "Property has an exchangeable value. Capital is property invested in business. Assets are available property."[66] Letters and numbers drifted lazily across the page.

While Tom was at the college, his sister Louise recalled:

> *One time he and a friend, Will Gracey rode up to Leith from Chatham on their bicycles. On their way up they came to a place where there was a garden party in full swing. Here was a chance for some fun and they decided to stop and help out with the programme. Tom had his mandolin along and they played and sang several songs. When they finished they passed a hat for a joke and were rather overwhelmed with the way the audience entered into the spirit of their prank.*[67]

In the fall of 1899, the South African Republic and Orange Free State declared war on Britain. In Canada, Lieutenant-Colonel William Dillon Otter called on all able men to fight the Boer in the Transvaal, "Where's the coward that dare not fight for such a queen?" Tom attempted to sign up but was rejected for flat feet—tough to take for a man that could hike twenty miles from Meaford to Leith.[68]

Along with "sailor," "soldier" is something Tom would never be. In his black-and-white mind, failure meant you were a failure; rejection meant you were a reject. As he struggled at the school where his siblings had succeeded, Tom internalized these experiences. His self-esteem taking hit, after hit, after hit.

Queen Victoria died early in 1901. Few alive had ever lived under another monarch's reign. Almost every building was embossed "Victoria Regina." More so than the usurped century, this is the end of an era. It was as Victoria had inscribed over the doors of Frogmore Mausoleum for her beloved Albert, *Vale desideratissime.* Farewell, most beloved.

That summer, Tom turned twenty-four. He joined brothers George and Henry who had settled in Seattle. There

Tom continued his education, studying penmanship at Acme Business College, which George owned and ran with his father-in-law. Tom did not volunteer his family connection to the other students. He kept his head down and focused on his studies, determined to succeed where he had not in Chatham.

George was now a single father, his wife having passed six years back. Not satisfied simply running the business school, George also earned a law degree at the University of Washington.

Tom stayed first with George, George's son and his in-laws. He studied during the day and worked nights as a liftboy at Diller's Hotel. One night, after a shift,

> *He was taking a short cut home…when suddenly there was a man came behind him and the first thing he knew he was looking down the barrel of a revolver and told to come across.*[69]
>
> *He held his hands up on the word and kept them up while the hold-up man, who, Tom said, was quite a young fellow, frisked him for a watch and four or five dollars. Tom was far the cooler of the two and remarked to the man who was robbing him that he must be new to the business as he trembled so violently. "Yes" said the bandit, "you are my first," and then, having secured everything of value Tom had on his person, he turned and bolted.*[70]
>
> *One of the boys said to him when he got home, "And what did you do Tommy?" Tom got up and in his own comical way, put his hands up and shook till his knees knocked together.*[71]

Tom found work, room and board with Charlie Maring, who had taught at Tom's business school back in Canada.

Maring was the proprietor of Maring and Ladd, the only complete engraving house north of San Francisco.

Tom's brother Fraser remembered: "He was very clever with pen and ink and secured a position with Maring and Ladd (later Maring and Blake Photo Engravers) as artist. It was not long before he could do the work of experienced artists."[72]

Commercial artist is an occupation Tom pursued until leaving to paint full time a decade later.

CHAPTER FOUR

Rocky Shore
Tom's False Start in Seattle

Seattle

Squeezed between Lake Washington and Elliott Bay, the city of seven hills: Jesus Christ Made Seattle Under Protest. Eighty thousand souls, the Klondike's dross, and the most bordellos per capita in the USA. That fall, the trial of Big John Considine, owner of half the box houses on Skid Row, the man who brought hoochie coochie and Little Egypt to town in ninety-nine. He shot Police Chief Meredith three times. The final shot so close his coat caught fire. The verdict returned: Not guilty."

At Maring and Ladd, Tom prepared the metal plates, the acrid smell of nitric acid etching zinc in his nose. In the anticipatory murk of the darkroom, Tom learned how tiny dots create an image, how three colours merge to make all others. Tom also learned how to wield shade, shadow and texture all to the buzz of scratching pens on paper.

According to Fraser:

> *Instead of his doing the work according to the instructions given by Mr. Maring he would invariably work out the design to suit his own ideas which would make Mr. Maring angry. During his stay with this concern there was not a single instance when a customer refused to accept his work.*[73]

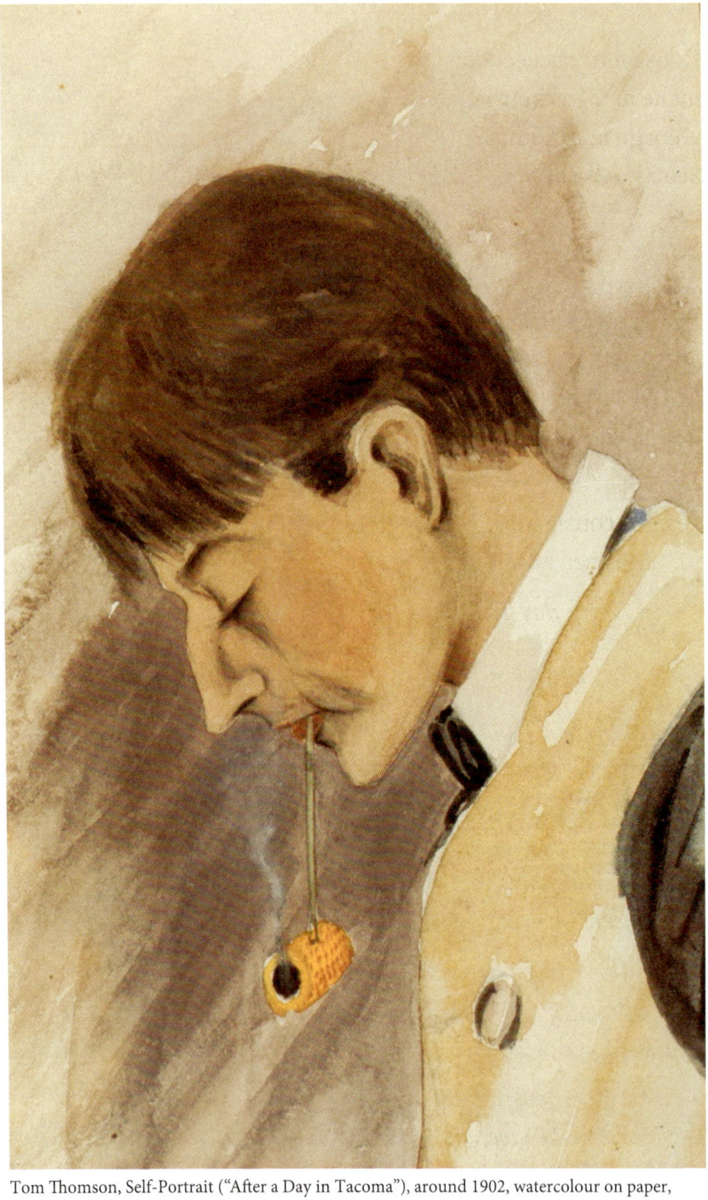

Tom Thomson, Self-Portrait ("After a Day in Tacoma"), around 1902, watercolour on paper, Collection of the Tom Thomson Art Gallery, Owen Sound

While President McKinley was slain, and Theodore Roosevelt succeeded, the Thomson children continued to make art. In their leisure time, Henry painted the mountains, George and Tom, the coast; Ralph, who joined his brothers in Seattle that winter, stuck with drawing. Many years later, Fraser and Margaret joined George in painting Ontario's Muskoka region,[74] adjoining the land their brother Tom would eventually make legendary.

Tom borrowed George's watercolours for a day trip. He returned with *After A Day in Tacoma, self-portrait*—head bowed, eyes closed, a wisp of smoke dancing on the bowl of his corncob pipe. He also worked in pen and ink, and black and white wash, copying ads from magazines, improving their design, consigning failed attempts to a mass grave.[75]

Another anecdote from brother Fraser:

> *One day Tom was sent over to the Seattle Engraving Co., Maring and Blake's strongest competitor. While there waiting to see Mr. Adams, he made a pencil sketch on the counter. Mr. Adams when he saw it asked Tom how much money he was getting and when told said that he would give $10.00 per week more if he would go to work for him. Tom accepted and went to work at once, but kept on boarding and rooming at Mr. Maring's house—void of any kind of fear.*[76]

When Ralph joined his brothers in Seattle, Tom found them both accommodations at The Shaws' boarding house. Ralph remembered:

> *Tom looked the family over from the front porch and decided they were o.k. And inside of the two minutes the room was rented. There were not two dozen words*

exchanged in the transaction, and he refused to even look at the room until we had our baggage moved.[77]

Tom roomed at Shaws' but continued to take his meals at Maring's, inviting Charlie over for evening get-togethers with his hosts and the other guests. Shaws' was an echo of Tom's busy house back home—the buzz of voices, footfalls and evenings around the piano and Tom's mandolin. Some evenings they went to the theatre: The Seattle, Third or Grand. Ralph remembered:

> *Whenever there was any good music at the theatres Tom and I were usually there—we nearly always were on hand early to rush the Gallery and get in the front row.* [78]

Weekends they would fish Elliott Bay, The Sound and Green Lake. Along with his rod and reel, Tom packed his sketchpad, pencils. It sometimes frustrated Ralph that, "Whenever an unusual scene showed up, I knew it was curtains as far as the fishing was concerned."[79]

Back at Shaws', Ralph watched Tom work:

> *I had a wonderful opportunity to observe his progress as a commercial artist and designer. He very often worked all night long while I watched him try one idea after another. The ones that did not meet with his approval he would either throw in the wastebasket, burn up or smear with cigar ashes or the ends of burned matches. Others he would keep for a day or two but they would invariably meet the same fate.*[80]

A decade later, Tom's friend Lawren Harris watched him flicking burnt matches into his oil paintings.[81] Here again the black-and-white thinking, the tyranny of perfection.

Alice Lambert, daughter of a Congregationalist minister, boarded weekends at Shaw's, rooming with Ralph's sweetheart Ruth Shaw. Years later, as a novelist she wrote:

> *For one disturbing year she had been desperately in love with a tall, dark boy named Tom, a commercial artist, who in the summer used to take her on street car rides to Alki Point and in the wintertime to the musty dimness of the Public Library where he would pore over prints and reproductions of the Masters.*[82]

Tom did take Alice out to Alki Point and the library, also dancing, her little warm hand in his, her fingers gently grazed his neck. They sang together back at Shaw's.[83]

> Harp and carp, Thomas, she said.
> Harp and carp, along wi' me,
> and if ye dare to kiss my lips,
> Sure of your bodie I will be! [84]

In Seattle, it seemed, Tom had everything he needed—family, friends, a career and a woman to share it with, but things did not go as he had hoped. Alice was independent and impulsive, and at eighteen not yet ready to settle down.

"Have I been strung along, played for a fool?" Tom agonized, "Does she really fancy Horace Rutherford instead of me?"[85]

When Tom realized where things stood, he packed up immediately and fled. But you can't flee failure, heartbreak.

> Now, ye maun go wi me, she said,
> True Thomas, ye maun go wi me,
> And ye maun serve me seven years,
> Thro weal or woe 'as may chance to be. [86]

Tom returned to Canada in the fall of 1904. He licked his wounds in Toronto, a discreet distance from his childhood home. There he worked at Legg Brothers photo engravers for a meagre eleven dollars a week[87] and boarded at Joseph Walton's on Elm Street near the Good Luck Athletic Club and The Women's Christian Temperance Union.[88]

Tom drank with his colleagues, his fellow boarders, sometimes alone. Sideways walking. Dawn vomit heave. At work, head in a vice. Dry eyes. Temples screaming. A wan silence. Muttered, "No patience for that nonsense today."

Tom Thomson Meets his Mentors

The year 1904 marked a low point in Thomson's life. After struggling to find a career and then to get through school, he finally found a place in Seattle with his brothers as a commercial artist, only to have heartbreak cause him to leave all that behind.

More tragic still, it seems Alice Lambert really did love Thomson. In a letter, decades after Thomson's death, Lambert recalled, "The street car stopped a mile away from the settlement on Alki, and we walked hand in hand, seldom speaking, my heart bursting with love—I have never felt toward anyone on earth as I did toward Tom."[89]

Despite the fact that Thomson's brother Ralph remained in Seattle, marrying the Shaws' daughter Ruth, Thomson and Lambert never wrote to each other. Lambert wrote, "I used to long to write him, or to find him, but a miserable experience prevented me."[90] I suspect Thomson's black-and-white thinking hindered him as well. With Thomson it was either, "she loves me, or she loves me not." In his mind, this failed romance made him a failure.

Hate, even when it is hate for one's self, is a weapon that injures the wielder, a sword without a hilt. Self-loathing is a feedback loop, and Thomson plumbed its depths after he left Seattle. This, not a sinister sphinx, was the demon that haunted Thomson until his death.

Thomson's early years in Toronto (1904–09), the "lost years" before he began working at The Grip Engravers with the future Group of Seven members, were sometimes grim ones. Legg Brothers co-worker Stuart L. Thompson noted Thomson "was very moody" and "subject to fits of depression which I think he played up largely."[91] And…there was the drinking.

"Occasionally he would drink too much when he would become morose and go home. Once he drank enough to quit and stayed away."[92]

It was during these lost years; however, that Thomson met the first of three mentors that would help him find his place, his land that he would work with paints instead of farm implements.

It is likely that Thomson had already met William Brodie, his grandmother's (Betty Thomson née Brodie) cousin at some point, but it was in Toronto that they began to spend significant amounts of time together. Because of their age difference—Brodie was older than Thomson's father—Tom called him Uncle William. It was also in Toronto where Brodie would explain the connection between man and nature that enabled Thomson to find his connection to his land. It was said of Brodie that he had, "not only the eye of the scientist, and of the artist, but his philosophical mind sought an explanation for what he saw."[93]

Then, as now, Toronto was a major urban center, packed with many neighborhoods rich and poor, but also riven with ravines, rivers and parks. It was in these green spaces that Thomson and Brodie walked for hours, observing nature. The green spaces were a welcome escape from the cramped boarding houses and the dirty and crowded neighborhoods in which Thomson lived and worked.[94]

The traditional view of Thomson's work that Professor Frye articulated is that the "unlived in" landscapes he painted had a sinister, even monstrous quality.[95] But this is exactly the opposite view Brodie likely would have held of Thomson's Algonquin Park or any other landscape for that matter.

Brodie embraced Charles Darwin's view that humans were an integral part of nature, not apart from it. Nature wasn't something outside of us; it was us. Even though Darwin had published his revolutionary ideas decades before, in the early 20th century it was far from being generally accepted or even understood.

Fast-forward a century or so to 2013. I was intrigued by the descriptions I'd read about Brodie, especially in Joan Murray's, *Tom Thomson: Design for a Canadian Hero.* Following a lead found in the notes, I made an appointment at the Royal Ontario Museum's archive. I penciled in my request for the William Brodie Fonds, donned my white cotton gloves and dug into the boxes full of papers when they arrived.

In amongst his articles on tree galls, insects and birds, I found his personal journal. Once I deciphered his handwriting, I saw that, rather than being full of personal appointments or daily reminiscences, it was filled with his philosophical musings. With a mixture of science and spiritualism, he pondered the meaning of life. Unlike most of us, he came up with some answers:

> *It is the aim and function of philosophy to construct intelligence out of nature—to construct nature out of intelligence—to express one in terms of the other and to demonstrate the harmony and unity of the two.*[96]

What I understand this to mean is that it is our purpose as intelligent beings, to understand our existence. We do this by constructing intelligence out of nature, which means observing the world around us—the landscape, of which we are an integral part—and building knowledge based on those observations. This is certainly what naturalists like Brodie did, but it applies to all branches of the sciences; think about Sir Issac Newton deducing the law of gravity by watching apples fall from a tree. I would further argue that the observation of nature is the basis of all the arts and sciences, all human enterprise. I think Brodie would, too.

We also understand our existence by constructing nature out of intelligence. We do this when we use the systems of thought and bodies of knowledge that arise from our observations of nature—the sciences and the arts—to understand the natural world around us.

Demonstrating the harmony between the two? This is the kicker for me. When we understand that the intelligence (the arts and the sciences), which we use to understand nature, itself arises from our observation of nature, we understand that there is no conflict between the two, between (human) intelligence and nature. There is harmony because one arises from the other and vice versa. There is harmony because, as Darwin explained, humans are an integral part of nature not apart from it. So what Brodie describes is Nature observing itself, understanding itself.

As I struggled to square Brodie's vision with Thomson's paintings, Frye's sphinx loomed large. Could this be the answer to the riddle of the Canadian sphinx? I decided that I had to gather more evidence before I confronted her with an answer.

For Thomson, a young man, an artist, who was desperately trying to find his place in the world, Brodie's vision would have been welcome indeed: Where do you belong? You belong right here, in the landscape around you. It would take another mentor to help Thomson find the tools to bring his vision to life and yet another to provide the means to enable him to paint full time, but with these essential pieces in place, Thomson was ready to discover his place, a land of his own.

CHAPTER FIVE

New Life After the Fire
Tom in Toronto

Toronto

Formerly York, a city sandwiched between rivers. Humber.
Don. A harbour bordered by a brace of islands. A flat land
fenced in by the shoreline of an ancient lake.
Slums circle the more affluent neighbourhoods. Conditions are
wretched, the sewers poor. Street boys hawk papers;
old women, pencils.
my old man is parailays no
Chiidlen we leve
in Toronto for
five year god blas you.
In 1904 a fire in the E&S neckwear plant razed one hundred
and twenty-four acres of warehouses from the railway up past
Wellington Street. Millions in damages, thousands out of work,
but only a single fatality. From guttered buildings
sprang arcades, broad banks of brick and stone, warehouses,
factories, commerce, community.

In the evenings Tom took drawing and painting lessons at the Central Ontario School of Art and Design near King and Simcoe. This intersection was known colloquially as the Nation's Four Corners. The buildings on each corner represented: Legislation, Education, Salvation and Damnation. Namely Government House, Upper Canada College, St. Andrew's Presbyterian, and the British Hotel and Tavern.

His teacher William Cruikshank, "a cantankerous old snorter," was rumoured to have taught Dana Gibson, creator of the ubiquitous Gibson Girl. Tom was working on Young Man with Team; it is dawn, a rural scene. A pair of horses confer quietly while a farmer contemplates the sunflower sky. "Did you paint this?" asked Cruikshank. A nod. "Well you'd better keep on.[97A]

Some weekends Tom visited his parents and siblings in Owen Sound. He visited Minnie at her finishing school in St. Catharines and made a watercolour sketch of St. Thomas', the church where they attended services.

Thy precious time misspent, redeem,
Each present day thy last esteem;
Improve thy talent with due care,
For the great day thyself prepare.[97B]

When Tom's brother Fraser visited Toronto, they watched the slumping Toronto Maple Leafs play baseball at Hanlan's Point, strolled along the boardwalk, "did King Street" on a Saturday night and caught the Mendelssohn Choir at Massey Hall.

In Toronto, thousands thronged to Union Station to see Tom Longboat, Canadian Winner of the Boston Marathon, fastest man on earth, running twenty-five miles in two hours, twenty-four minutes, twenty-four seconds. The crowd carried him to City Hall. Mayor Coatsworth pinned a medal to his chest. Years later, not so fast, he would sweep the streets he was carried through, fame fleeter than the fastest foot-runner.

On Sundays, Tom walked with his grandmother's favourite cousin, William Brodie, director of the Biology Department of the Provincial Museum. They would walk by his house along the Don River, where prisoners from the Central Jail would milk his four cows, or out to the Scarborough Bluffs, or through the Black Oak forest in High Park. "They burned out all the trailing arbutus, damn them!" Brodie fumes.

On their walk, Brodie expounded:

> *It is the aim and function of philosophy to construct intelligence out of nature—to construct nature out of intelligence—to express one in terms of the other and to demonstrate the harmony and unity of the two.*[98]
>
> *You see Tommy, it's our job to make sense of the natural world, the world we are an integral part of. We do that by reconstructing it, using science and art. And because we are a part of nature, not apart from it, we thereby make sense of ourselves. You see?*

Although he had no formal training as a biologist, Brodie collected tens of thousands of specimens: plants, insects, animals. He donated the lot in exchange for his appointment at the museum,[99] release from his day job as a dentist.

Not apart, but a part of the land that surrounds them, they found specimens for Brodie's collection. Tom snapped shots with his Brownie, sketched on the *Imitation Steinbach* pages of his *Watercolour Sketcher's Pocket Book*.

Brodie told him, "The beginning of wisdom is the knowing of names: staghorn sumac, paper birch, red maple, white pine."

One Sunday, Brodie told Tom about his recent expedition to Algonquin Park, the establishment of which was partly to Brodie's credit, "The bare gneiss glacier-worn rock, high, irregular. Precipitous hillsides. Broken rocky ridges. Lumbered already of profitable pine, and the slashings much burned-over. There is a fine overgrowth of young maple, beech, red oak and white pine."[100] Tom recalled Brodie's description when he first visited the park seven years later.

In 1906, Tom's brother George saw a fine, modern, colourful picture, "a seascape of the California coast: rocks, cliffs and rolling sea"[101] displayed in a Seattle shop window. For George, this picture was a thunderclap, a shooting star, a starving saint. It awakened in George the ambition to paint professionally. George became the first Thomson to declare himself a painter. At thirty-eight, he sold his business and took his young son to New York, joining the Art Students League.

Within the year, George's work was shown at the National Academy of Design and the Art Institute of Chicago. For George, success, satisfaction, came early.

At twenty-nine, Tom—turned out nattily in silk shirt, peg-top pants and horned shoes—danced at the Centre Island pavilion and the ballroom of the Gladstone Hotel with Elizabeth "Arty" McCarnen. Together they explored the Art Museum and the Fine Art Building at the Canadian National Exhibition. At "the Ex" they also visited a sideshow exhibit: an "African Village."

Zulus, Matabeles, Swazies and
th African tribes clad in their

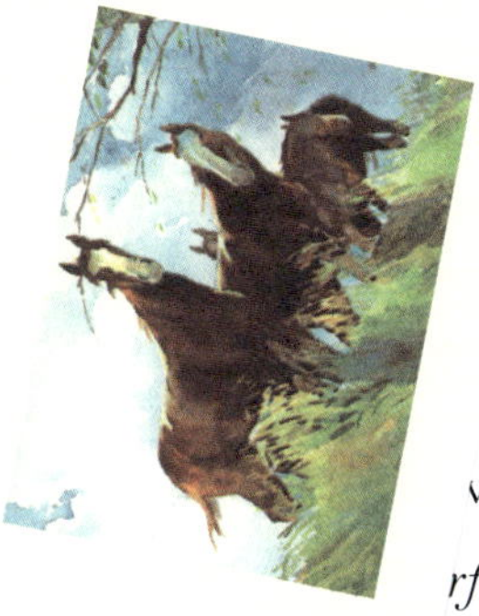

Tom. He revisited it again and
were truly a part of their environ-
inhabitants, boarding house ten-
ot all, of the villagers were likely
ited from the vaudeville circuit.
visited Toronto. She recalled:

rful visit together. He knew the most
and one day he took me to McKon-
there before, and remarked on what
was, how cool and restful, and on the
d delicious food, and Tom said, "I would
ays, but one can't on $15 a week." (That
was wh... 'd when he came to Toronto.) [103] *After a while he said, "I like the atmosphere of this place, and the class of people who come here."*

I wonder if any of his artist friends ever suspected [Tom's] *hunger for the refinements and niceties of life. His choosing of the more primitive mode of living was rather of necessity than preference.*[104]

September 2, 1908, crowds lined the Scarborough Beach boardwalk as Charles F. Willard and his Golden Flyer biplane took off over the lake. After a few minutes flying at an altitude of several feet, the plane splashed into the water. Three more attempts; three more crashes. Willard returned to the States.

Back at Legg, Tom tired of the get-by attitude, of the hacks, the clock-watchers. Although he had taken his sister Minnie to the office and introduced her to his co-workers,[105] he had stopped caring about the work. One day he overheard two designers complaining they're underpaid, that many shops paid five dollars a week more. Tom put together his portfolio and did the rounds.

That winter, Tom showed his bundle of work to Albert Robson, art director of The Grip, a rival photo engraving shop.

> *A tall, lanky young man in a dark blue serge suit and grey flannel shirt applied for a position in the art department of Grip. He was clean cut, almost classical in features, with a mop of black hair combed down over his right forehead. There was something intriguing about Thomson, a quiet reserve, a reticence almost approaching bashfulness. There was no bombast or assertiveness as he handed me a bundle of his work and asked if there was an opening in the art department.*
>
> *His samples consisted mostly of lettering and decorative designs applied to booklet covers and some labels. A quick glance at his drawings revealed something more than mechanical and technical proficiency; there was a feeling for spacing and arrangement, an over-tone of intellectual as well as aesthetic approach to his work, and we quickly closed arrangement for him to join the staff.*[106]

His work was proficient and promising enough to win him a position under the kindly supervision of J.E.H. MacDonald. Although MacDonald was only a few years older, Tom called him Mr. MacDonald and would do so the rest of his life.

About this time, Robson received a phone call about Tom:

> *Shortly after hiring him I received a gratuitous and unsolicited phone call from his previous employer belittling Thomson as an erratic and difficult man in a department.*
>
> *This was as absurd as it was untrue. Thomson was a most diligent, reliable and capable craftsman. Nothing seemed to disturb the even tenor of his way.*[107]

Clearly, Robson had not talked to Stuart L. Thompson, Tom's former colleague at Legg Brothers. But in any case, by all descriptions, it seems Tom had turned over a new leaf at his new job.

The Grip's Art Room had a schoolhouse scheme of desks laid out in rows—rows of celluloid collars, neckties and waistcoats. Suspended in a blue haze of tobacco, was the thrum of male voices, scratching pens. MacDonald's desk was a tangle of sketches, pens, brushes and books with a corner clear for working.

At first Tom was an inconspicuous presence: quiet, hard-working, and at 31, older than everyone in the department, save MacDonald and Robson. He watched but did not join the horseplay: wrestling, stamping, kicking and hanging from the steam pipes.[108] He smoked his pipe—feculent smoke issuing from his Hudson Bay tobacco[109]—laid Ben Day tints on metal plates, did some lettering.

> *When more arrogant souls despised the Ben Day (and incidentally were no good at running it) Thomson took it in his stride. Aware of his undoubted and varied skills, he never threw his weight around as do those who feel inferior. It was not beneath his dignity to attend those jobs calling for Ben Day shading. He had no wisecracks to*

> *offer, no prescription for the Good Life, nor any particular philosophy of life. The phrase "inferiority complex" had hardly yet come into use.*[110]

Tom's silence was matched by the silence of MacDonald. Silence seemed to grow around MacDonald. It was not willful, nor forced or assumed priestly.[111] Tom found it impossible to knock heads with MacDonald or Robson. Both were encouraging, patient and kind. His co-workers in the Art Room were a motley bunch: Frank Johnston, an irreverent joker and his brother Bob; Harry Jackson, an avid angler who'd fished much of the East Coast; Tom MacLean, who'd worked as a prospector and fire ranger up north; and Stanley "Kempus" Kemp, an intellectual who had studied to be a minister.

Coincidently, Kemp would one day become the father-in-law of the very same Northrop Frye who would write the influential interpretation of Thomson's work.

Tom's sister Minnie offered a dissenting opinion on Tom's silence:

> *One opinion which seems to be held by most of Tom's friends is that he was unusually reserved and quiet. I can't somehow reconcile that description of him with the Tom we all knew and loved at home. He had his quiet moods but one never caught his glance but he would smile...With his own folk he was not reserved and silent. He dearly loved an argument and generally held his own in a battle of wits.*[112]

Tom moved to Esther Plewes' boarding house at 99 Gerrard Street East to be closer to the office, and there befriended Med student John "Doc" McRuer and Edgar Burke, an engineer at the CNR. So close was their friendship that Tom was best man at both their weddings the following year.[113]

As he stood in the nave, at the chancel's edge, watching Doc watch his bride walk up the aisle, Tom's heart was full: "If I can be so filled with joy on behalf of others, surely that joy resides in me, the possibility of joy, the potential."

While Commander Peary doggedly sought The North Pole and the University of Toronto Varsity Blues won the inaugural Stanley Cup, Tom's beloved uncle, William Brodie died, one day after Tom's 32nd birthday, August 6, 1909. As J.E.H. MacDonald would one day write on Tom's cairn, Nature "...took him to itself." Tom's girlfriend Arty also left Tom's life that year, returning to Phelpston, Ontario, to care for her brother Bernard's children, he having recently passed away.

In March 1910, Tom and his brother Fraser, who was now working as a haberdasher in Montreal, attended the Ontario Society of Artists exhibition at Toronto's central library. Both Tom's co-workers, J.E.H. MacDonald and Frank Johnston, had paintings there. When Fraser admired one painting, Tom shot back, "How far away would these trees be? You see the veins on the leaves? Could you make out that detail from that distance? No."[114]

That Monday, back at The Grip, MacDonald raved about the work of a Montrealer, A.Y. Jackson, but Tom had been most impressed by the work of a Toronto artist, J.W. Beatty, *The Evening Cloud of the Northland.* The image of a distant shore atop an expansive lake, massive clouds in a widesome sky, was burned into Tom's inner eye, a template for the works he would shortly paint.

In May, Tom and his co-worker Harry Jackson left typhoid-ridden Toronto behind and headed up to Huntsville to fish and visit Tom's old housemate, Doc McRuer. On the northbound train, Tom watched the terrain blur by, the blasted bedrock, cross-sectioned for the railway, looking like nothing so much as raw meat.

> *Tom eagerly took the McRuer brothers (Doc and his younger brother Jim, a lawyer) to his room in the Dominion Hotel where, "he opened his pack and excitedly spread out on the bed four feet of his brilliant sketches. The air in the room was heady with the scent of oil paints."*[115]

On May 6, Queen Victoria's son Edward died, and his son George succeeded, another era's end. About this time, William Broadhead joined The Grip from Sheffield, England, all confidence, bravado and pride, followed shortly by his friend Arthur Lismer. They were both *figure men* with European art school educations. Blithe Lismer was nicknamed "The Bronc," an immigrant unbroken to Canadian culture.

An apprentice was also hired that year, a thin, bespectacled, twenty-one-year-old carriage painter from Orillia named Franklin Carmichael. MacDonald and Tom took him under their wings. They sent him off to Tom's old teacher, Cruikshank, for evening lessons.

Back in his boarding house, in his room, Tom sketched the corner store across the street again and again. Damnation. Immolation. Wastebasketing failures.[116]

In 1911, spring brought the OSA exhibition once again. Tom's workmates Johnson, MacLean, MacDonald and Lismer all had work in the show. This time MacDonald and Tom agreed A.Y. Jackson's *The Edge of the Maple Wood* was the standout piece. The shadow of an unseen tree falls through the foreground pulling the viewer into the scene, they become a part of the scene, not apart from it.

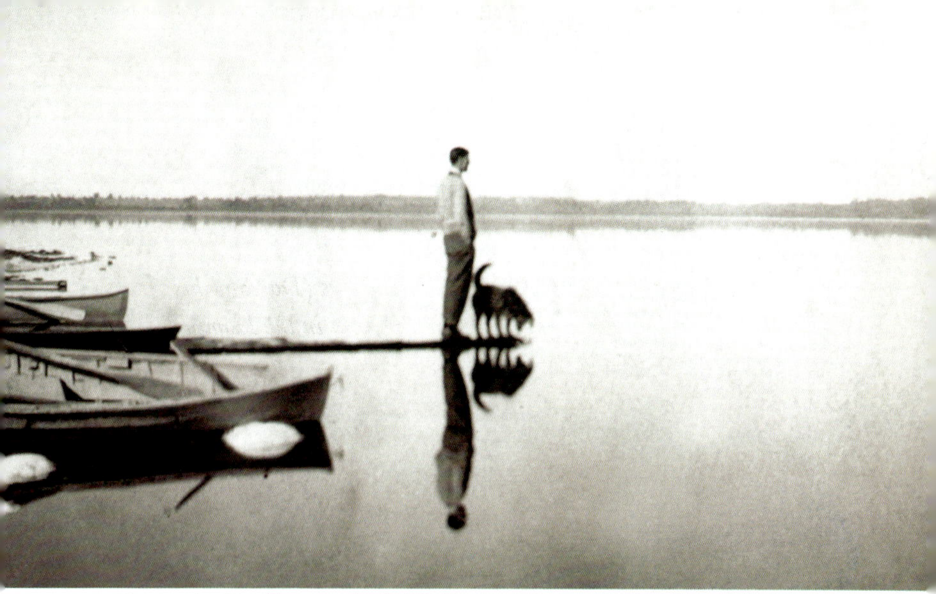

Photograph of Tom Thomson taken by T.H. Marten at Lake Scugog in the fall of 1910.
Collection of the Tom Thomson Art Gallery

> When seven years were come and gane,
> The sun blink'd fair on pool and stream;
> And Thomas lay on Huntlie bank,
> Like one awaken'd from a dream.[117]

With both his uncle and Arty gone, Tom began to go sketching with the gang from The Grip. They went to nearby Weston, Lambton Mills and York Mills.[118] He heeded, finally, MacDonald's fiat: *nulla dies sine linea*. Not a day without drawing a line.[119]

That summer, Tom got his first sketch box. Designed to sit on one's knees, the combination easel/palette held paint tubes and brushes, and had slots to keep the sketch boards apart, allowing air to circulate around them.

Picture this: Tom uses only three or four colours. A few squeezes from each tube. He paints quickly, remembering MacDonald's mantra: Tone. Rhythm. Balance. Harmony.

For Tom, progress was slow...glacial. One outing by the Humber River, after seeing the successful work of his companions, Tom paced in frustration, unable to translate from his mind to his brush and board. "Dammit!" He pitched his whirling panel into the bush.[120]

Back at The Grip, MacDonald reviewed all proffered boards, parceling out praise and advice. He himself did not join the "sketchpeditions," preferring his own company, and that of his wife and young son, Thoreau.

Tom sketched throughout the summer, going farther afield to Lindsay and Lake Scugog with Harry Jackson,[121] *'lunge* fishing, with his mandolin as distraction, entertainment, medication. Tom sang, "I dwelt alone in a world of moan, and my soul was a stagnant tide, 'till the fair and gentle Eulalie became my blushing bride."[122]

Jackson recalled:

> *"He cared nothing for social life, but with one or two companions on a sketching & fishing trip with his pipe and Hudson Bay Tobacco going, was a delightful companion. If a party or the boys got a little loud or rough, Tom would get his sketching kit & wander off alone.*[123]

On visits to Leith, Tom entertained his nephews and nieces, painting ferocious tigers as they sat rapt on the arms of his chair. George and his son visited too. George, living then in Old Lyme artists' colony in New Haven, criticized Tom's sketch. By the next morning, Tom had redrawn it.[124]

In the OSA of 1912, MacDonald showed with Lawren Harris, with whom he'd been painting over the winter—somber cityscapes of Toronto's Ward neighborhood, a place of "filth and disorder," squalid and contemptible.[125] Lismer and

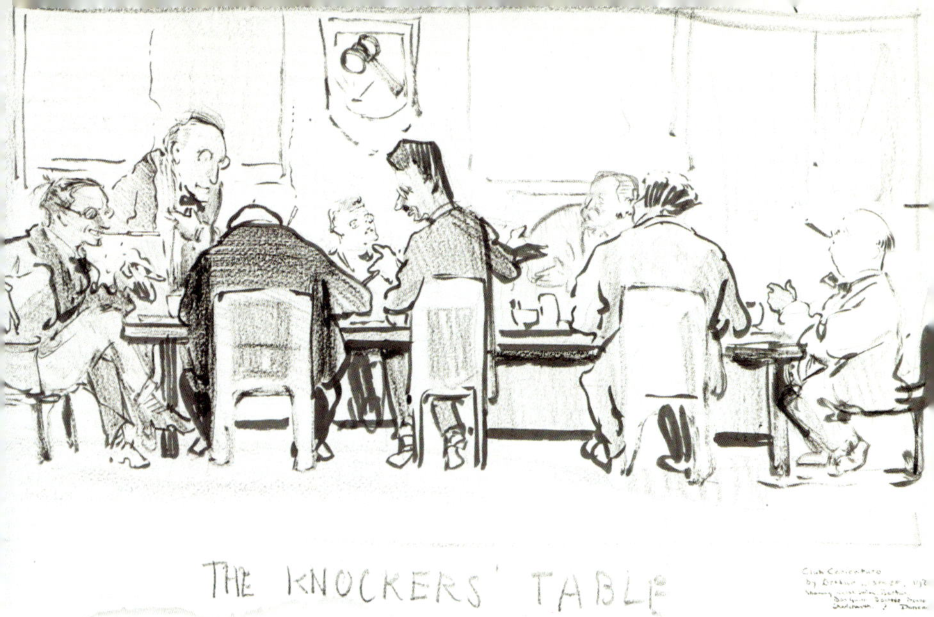

Arthur Lismer, *The Knocker's Table,* 1922, charcoal and/or conté crayon on paper laid down on paperboard, McMichael Canadian Art Collection

Broadhead were also represented, and Carmichael showed for the first time.

Tom took lunch with his Gripmates at the Arts and Letters Club,[126] that "most inaccessible of rooms." The entrance was through a dark, foul-smelling alley behind police headquarters. A manure pile and a pile of firewood were a *Scylla and Charybdis* for members, who were expected to haul in a snow-covered stick from off the pile on their way in.[127] There Tom and his friends dined at the Art Table, across from the "Knockers" Table where critics Gadsby and Charlesworth sat. Relations were civil, bad reviews being better than no reviews at all.

After years of graft and scandal, Premier Whitney finally brought Niagara power to the people of Toronto. With an audience of forty thousand, he pushed the button that lit the city. At City Hall a replica of the falls was activated. Malfunctioning, it soaked the unsuspecting onlookers.

While the doomed *Titanic* foundered and *Seward's Folly*, Alaska, attained statehood, MacDonald—Tom's mentor and silent supporter—left The Grip to paint full-time at Harris' urging. MacDonald had a patron in Dr. MacCallum, a wealthy oculist and Arts and Letters Club member who had treated Tom's uncle, William Brodie.[128]

In May 1912, after listening all winter to his co-worker Tom MacLean spin stories of "up north," Tom took a leave from The Grip to take two trips. The first, a few months in Algonquin Park camping and fishing with Harry Jackson.

Picture this: The two men board the Grand Trunk train car at Union Station, climbing out of the sewage stink and smoky skies of Toronto. After six tedious hours, they emerge into the pleasant purgatory of Scotia Junction to picnic with Doc McRuer and friends—up from nearby Huntsville—before transferring to the Ottawa, Arnprior and Parry Sound line on their way to Canoe Lake Station.[129]

Park Ranger Mark Robinson met Tom and Jackson at the station: they had a letter of introduction for Park Superintendent George Bartlett from MacLean in hand.[130]

> *I was detailed to watch Joe Lake Station and Canoe Lake Station. We were to take the names of such persons as got off at the stations—find out their destination, the time they would spend in the Park, and also what they were going to do. We'd find that out and assist them in every way we could and also if it became necessary, search their*

> *packs to find if they* [were] *trappers proceeding under disguise of such persons.*
>
> *One evening as I went to Canoe Lake, a couple of Rangers had joined me, and we went down to Canoe Lake and as the train came in, drew to a stop, a tall, fine-looking young man with a packsack on his back stepped off the train. "There's your man," someone said to me. I saw at once that the man was not the man we were after."*[131]

After they were cleared as poachers, Tom asked about accommodations.

> *He inquired where he could get a good bed and good "eats," as he called it, good meals. Well, I explained to him that the Algonquin Hotel was a short distance away, about a quarter of a mile, and also that there was Mowat Lodge about a mile and a half distance—there was a man by the name of Fraser at a stopping place known as Mowat Lodge where he could get good meals and excellent beds.* [Tom said] *"I think that's the place for me. How far did you say?" "Mile and a half," and I said, "Mr. Fraser's right here, I will introduce him to you."*[132]

Fraser was hired by Gilmour Lumber Company to dismantle their mill after logging operations went bust. He stayed on, converting bunkhouse to inn, a seasonal home to nature lovers, sportsmen and American tourists.

Fraser told Tom and Jackson, "Well, I think we can make room for you, we're pretty well filled but we'll try and provide some room for you some place."[133] In fact, they only had two other guests.[134] The men loaded their gear into Fraser's cart, and they clip-clopped along the tree-shadowed dirt lane roadway to Mowat Lodge

Tom Thomson Finds His Way

With the help of William Brodie, J.E.H. MacDonald and his friends from The Grip, Thomson managed to overcome the demon of self-loathing born from his past failures, romantic and professional. He had a job he enjoyed and started going on sketching expeditions into the green spaces of Toronto and beyond to paint landscapes with his friends.

Thomson shared Brodie's vision of humans as an integral part of nature, not apart from it, and would begin to process this concept through his art.

It was at this time that something happened. It's nothing I've ever read a satisfying explanation of. Nothing, certainly, that Thomson wrote about, and if he told anyone about it, we have no record. Something happened on Thomson's trip to Algonquin Park that caused him to keep coming back to paint it every year until his death.

Thomson's companion in Algonquin, Harry Jackson, said that Tom only really started to paint after (not during) their trip,

> *Prior to* [Thomson's sketching trip to Mississagi] *Tom's oils were mostly notes or thumb-box sketches. I do not think he ever had the idea his work would ever be taken seriously, in fact he used to chuckle over the idea.*[135]

Although Thomson may have fished more than he painted on their Algonquin trip,[136] when he chose a place to paint, he did not go back to Northern Ontario, back to Biscotasing where he sketched with his Grip coworker William Broadhead or to Georgian Bay where he would sketch at the invitation of Dr. James MacCallum, his future benefactor. Thomson went back to Algonquin Park, again and again. But why?

Aside from being close to Huntsville, where his friend Doc McRuer lived, Algonquin Park was also a place where William Brodie had visited. In fact, William Brodie was involved in the establishment of Algonquin Park.

When Thomson saw the Algonquin landscape, he thought of his uncle. He saw there a vital landscape that had been changed by human enterprise but was no less vital for those changes. Or, as poet A.J.M. Smith wrote in *The Lonely Land*, "This is the beauty/ of strength/ broken by strength/ and still strong." Although Brodie was dead, Thomson could feel close to him by visiting the landscape Brodie had visited, painting the park he had helped to establish. It was here, in this landscape that had been changed by humans, that Thomson felt an integral part of nature. It was here he could "construct nature out of intelligence" by painting vibrant portraits of a vital landscape in which we belonged, of which we were an integral part.

I was one step closer to the riddle of the Canadian sphinx, but another puzzle piece remained missing.

CHAPTER SIX:

In the Northland
Tom Discovers Algonquin Park

Mowat

In 1896 the village of Mowat sat
on the northwest shore of Canoe Lake. The Gilmore
Lumber Company Mill employed most of
the six hundred inhabitants. Three years later—bypassed
by the Ottawa-Parry Sound line, park headquarters set up
on Cache Lake—the mill closed, the people left. Mowat became
a name without a village. A collection of abandoned
buildings and a ruined mill. A small graveyard with two tenants:
an infant and a young lumberjack, his marker carved by a friend:
"Remember comrade as you pass by
As you are now so once was I
As I am now so you will be
Prepare thyself to follow me."
Hardly a northern enclave, Algonquin Park shares latitude
with Venice, Milan, Bordeaux. But here north
is an idea, like wild, free."

Tom and Jackson spent the night at the lodge before setting out. They portaged Canoe Lake to Bonita to South Tea.

Harry Jackson recalled,

> *Tom was a real cook…our lake trout was boiled & baked not fried, real biscuits etc. Everything had to be cooked just so. If it was a rainy day we would stay in camp. Tom would clean his pipes and read Walton's Compleat Angler.*[137]

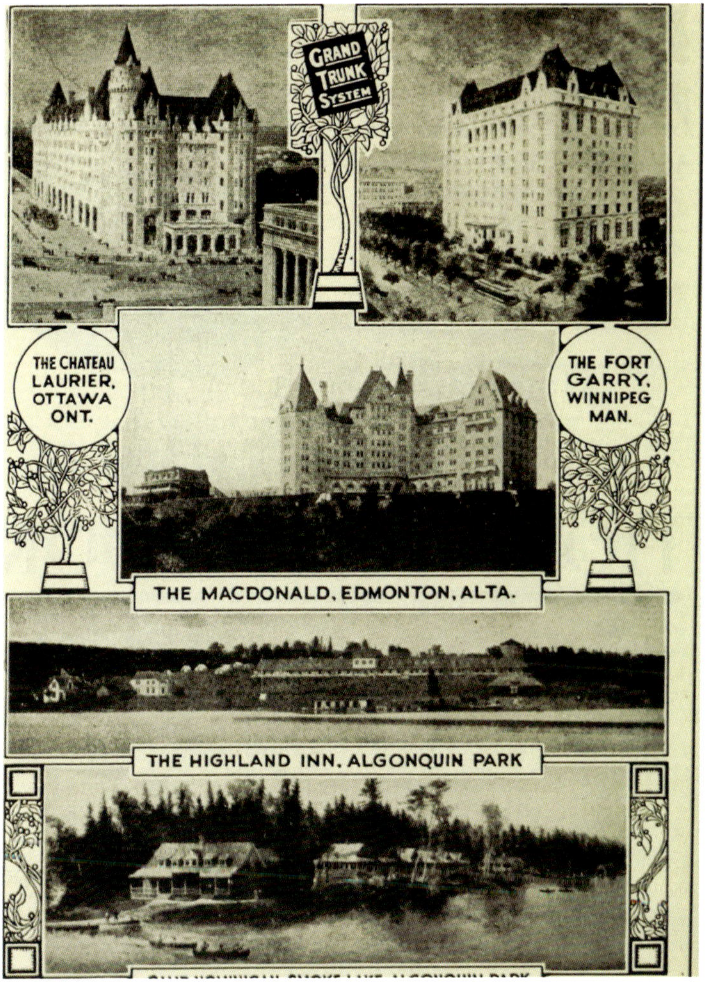

The *Official Hotel Red Book and Directory*, 1903, Allen County Public Library Genealogy Center

"And upon all that are lovers of virtue; and dare trust in his providence; and be quiet; and go a-angling."[138]

> *It was one of those days I made a portrait sketch. Deer visited the camp every eve. Wolves could be heard in the distance.*[139]

Tom agreed to take some tourists, Leonard Mack and Harry Bracken, trout fishing on Crown Lake. That evening, as he prepared to depart, a storm was brewing. Shannon Fraser, recognizing his inexperience, advised him to wait until tomorrow. "For God's sake, don't say anything to them." Tom begged, "I'm their guide!"[140]

At Molly Lake, Park Ranger Bud Callighen saw Tom sketching. He stood waiting to be acknowledged. Waited, waited. After about ten minutes, without turning, "Howdy," said Tom. "Howdy," said Callighen.[141]

By the trip's end, Tom had painted fewer than a dozen sketches, including *Northern Lake, Thunderhead, Old Lumber Dam* and *Smoke Lake, Algonquin Park.* The latter made at Nominigan Point—Tom's somber palette plus a rich blue swath of sunny sky on lake. Callighen so admired the sketch that Tom made him a gift of it.

Back in Toronto, Tom moved in temporarily with William Broadhead and Art Lismer at their Summerhill digs.[142] Lismer was about to head back to Sheffield to marry. He introduced Tom to Fred Varley, another figure man from Sheffield. Animus and angst, all aimed outwards, Varley was a mop of fiery red hair in corduroy, an intemperate drinker, and though married, a womanizer.

"If I am weak at times and seem to fail you—it is not that my love is less—just that I am weak."[143]

Varley lived out his tempers, temptations, whereas Tom's passions were largely self-contained. They became fast friends.

In August, Tom and Broadhead caught the Canadian Pacific main line to Bisco, north of Elliot Lake. There they met Archie Belaney, ranger, Englishman, liar, his face burned "black as the arse of a tea kettle." He posed as part Cherokee, part Scots and quoted Shakespeare, especially when drunk. He was impressed with Tom's donuts, fried in fat over an open fire. Belaney would be run out of Bisco later that year after taking shots at the church bell on a Sunday during services.[144]

Belaney, in his guise as the Indigenous naturalist Grey Owl, would have agreed with Frye's appraisal of the landscape if not Thomson's paintings of it. He wrote about the, "brooding relentless evil spirit of the Northland,"[145] which undoubtedly made his alleged exploits more impressive.

Tom and Broadhead bought their supplies from the Hudson's Bay store: flour, sugar, pork, beans, rice, prunes, baking powder, desiccated potatoes, onions, milk. They departed just as a group of "aristocrats" were packing up their gear.

> *"Mr. Broadhead said a party of English aristocrats started in from Bisco after they left, taking with them camp beds, chairs, carpet slippers, table napkins and other civilized luxuries, but how they have fared since he does not know, but can easily imagine."* [146]

Tom and Broadhead canoed three hundred miles under heavy skies, from Spanish River to the Mississagi River, Aubrey Falls. At Green Lake they were held up for several days by a rainstorm. A sudden cloudburst swamped their canoe and threw them into the water, wetting their blankets and provisions.

Picture this: Wood smoke bites at the back of their throats. They pick bones from the plentiful pike and sleep in soggy tents. At Clear Lake, they come across a washout, a tent, but no people. They search for fire rangers but find only sand beneath sand.

They were dumped again on Forty Mile Rapids—the rush of white water, sunken rocks, and dozens of rolls of film and several sketches snatched by the river. Just as the biggest fish get away so the best sketches always drown.

Tom and Broadhead paddled on to Squaw Chute and came down by way of the Soo to Owen Sound.[147]

Back in Leith, Tom's brother-in-law, Jim Henry asked him,

> *"Are you not afraid to be so much alone with so many wild animals roaming about?" "Why," he said, "the animals are our friends. I've picked raspberries on one side of a log while a big black bear picked berries on the other side."*
>
> [Tom] *also told* [Jim Henry] *of one time he was tramping through the woods when he heard some animal coming towards him through the undergrowth and to his surprise it was a large timber wolf, one of the largest he had ever seen, its head, neck and breast were jet black and the body the usual grey color. He said it was the most beautiful animal he had ever seen.*[148]

Tom told Jim Henry,

> *He sniffed me up and down and apparently decided I was alright, so he turned and went his way, and I went*

mine. Do you know Jim, I only tell that story to those who know me well. I told it to some folk in Toronto, and the look they gave me was enough.[149]

Tom returned to Toronto and discovered that his boss, Albert Robson, had left The Grip for Rous & Mann Press, taking most of the department with him. Lismer, like MacDonald before him, had left to paint full-time, and Tom MacLean stayed at The Grip being "too lazy a devil to move."[150]

Still in his *mackinaw* trousers and flannel shirt, Tom visited Rous & Mann unannounced, a bundle of sketches in hand.[151] In MacDonald's absence, Robson commented on the improvement of Tom's technique and the "purity of his colour."[152]

Shortly afterwards, MacDonald introduced Thomson to his patron, Dr. MacCallum.

It was in October 1912 that I first met him—in the studio of J.E.H. MacDonald. The door opened and in walked a tall, slim, clean cut, dark young chap who was introduced to me as Tom Thomson. Quiet, reserved, chary of words. he interested me, for I had heard of his adventures in the [Mississagi] *Forest Reserve. I asked MacDonald to get some of his sketches so that I might get an idea of what the country is like.*

This was done, and I realized their truthfulness, their feeling and their sympathy with the grim, fascinating northland. Dark they were, muddy in colour, tight, and not wanting in technical defects, but they made me feel that the North had gripped Thomson, as it had gripped me ever since, when a boy of eleven, I first sailed and paddled through its silent places.[153]

MacCallum bought *Old Lumber Dam, Algonquin Park* and a few others. Of his first sale, his initiation as a professional painter, Tom said, "Thanks, that will let me buy some more paint."[154] "Some hae meat and canna eat."[155]

Later that month, Tom followed Robson and the others to Rous & Mann. After hearing many stories about Tom's trips and seeing some of the sketches, Robson pressed Tom to paint up a proper canvas.

"We urged him to paint one of his sketches upon a large canvas and gave him the keys and use of the studio on week-ends."[156]

In the winter of 1912, at the age of 35, Tom began work on his first full-size canvas, *Northern Lake.* Little sketches, dashed off in a moment, are easily excused. Easily erased, tossed aside. But a canvas is a statement, a declaration, on show for friends and critics alike. Tom's mind squirmed, "Still, I've agreed to work at the shop. They're all expecting to see something, even young Carmichael has exhibited. George has many paintings, shown, sold."

Tom painted and repainted. Transposing board to canvas requires more than copying. MacDonald visited, advising Tom to add a foreground, something to get the viewer to look into the picture. Tom added boulders, brush. But the boulders weren't right. Varley suggested whorls, vortices, and showed Tom how to mix a thin wash of oil paint and turpentine, and paint and then paint over using his palette knife.[157]

That winter, both Tom's travel companions, Harry Jackson and Bill Broadhead, decamped for more profitable pastures in the U.S.A. MacDonald and Harris, inspired by an exhibition of Scandinavian art at the Albright Gallery in Buffalo—the bold and forceful handling of the snow!—began

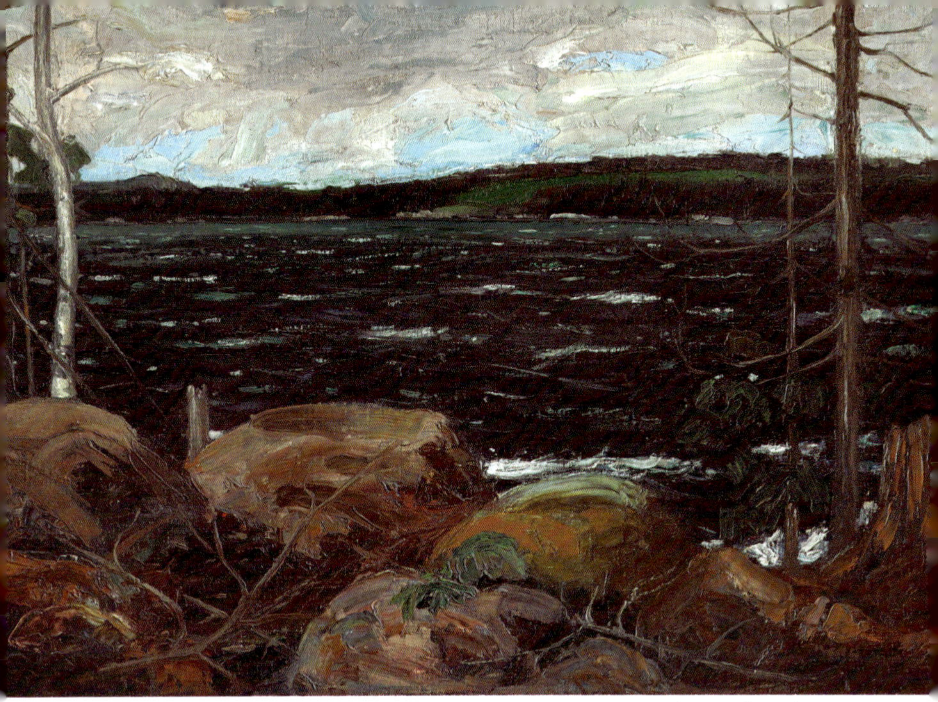

Tom Thomson, *Northern Lake,* 1912–1913, The Tom Thomson Collection at the Art Gallery of Ontario

to speak of a national school of painting. They organized an "Exhibition of Little Pictures" by Canadian painters of Canadian subjects. Invited were the usual suspects from The Grip, and Arts and Letters Club, plus A.Y. Jackson and Maurice Cullen from Montreal. Tom did not participate.

At the OSA of 1913, however, Tom did show his canvas, *Northern Lake.* He was joined by Harris, MacDonald and the rest of The Grip group, A.Y. Jackson and Arts & Letters alumni Art Heming, C.W. Jefferys and J.W. "Bill" Beatty, whose *Evening Cloud of Northland* Tom had so admired. Tom's brother George also sent a canvas up from Connecticut where he was now living.

The Year Book of Canadian Art, 1913 [158]

Tom Thomson's *"Northern Lake"* is remarkable for its fidelity to the northern shore; boulders and undergrowth in the foreground, the brown water turned to the deep blue of the sky under the fresh gale that is putting white caps on the little lake.

To Harris, Tom's canvas was the work of a natural, one born to paint, having vision, lacking only technique, craft. Harris felt antithetical, with his European art school education, theories and creeds in abundance lacking only the vision. The how, lacking the what, not knowing the why. "Some wad eat that want it."[159]

Tom lived then at Mrs. McKenzie's boarding house at 61 Breadalbane Street. He shared many lunch counter meals with Varley—dinners of Chop Suey and Souvlaki sandwiches—until Fred Varley's wife Maud and the children arrived in April. Once they were settled, the Varleys treated Tom like a member of the family.

"There was a cot bed always ready for him whenever he felt like staying."[160]

Feeling Tom was "very lonely,"[161] Fred Varley tried to set Tom up with his wife's half-sister, Dora. Although Dora liked Tom, he balked at the match, "I'm not fit for a good girl, Fred. I'm a wild man."[162]

One day in May, Tom at his desk at Rous and Mann, Albert Robson walked over grinning, "Tom, your painting has been bought!" As he continued to work, Tom's neck reddened, "What damn fool did that?"[163] he muttered.

Tom and Lismer, whose *The Clearing* had also been bought, cashed their cheques for 250 one-dollar bills—half a year's salary! Back at Lismer's digs on Wellesley Street, they tossed the money into the air and danced a fandango. Later, Tom pinned his money to the wainscoting of his room just to see it all together at once.[164]

All that spring, Tom plotted his return to the north, to the scent of balsam fir, to the breaking buds, the blossoms, marshy bogs, the plentiful trout and bass.

"One day Tom came into work carrying a canoe paddle. He filled a photographer's tank with water and put it beside his chair; then, without a word, he sat there gently paddling. At each stroke he gave a real canoeman's twist." [165]

When the spring came, Tom headed up, not to Algonquin, but north of Bisco, where he'd canoed the year before, to Mattagami to do some fire ranging. It was late in the summer when Tom returned to Canoe Lake. The smell of the water, the sound of the wind in the trees, greeted him like old friends. He set up camp at Hayhurst Point, across the lake from Mowat Lodge—Hudson Bay blankets, pots, pans, a sack of flour.[166]

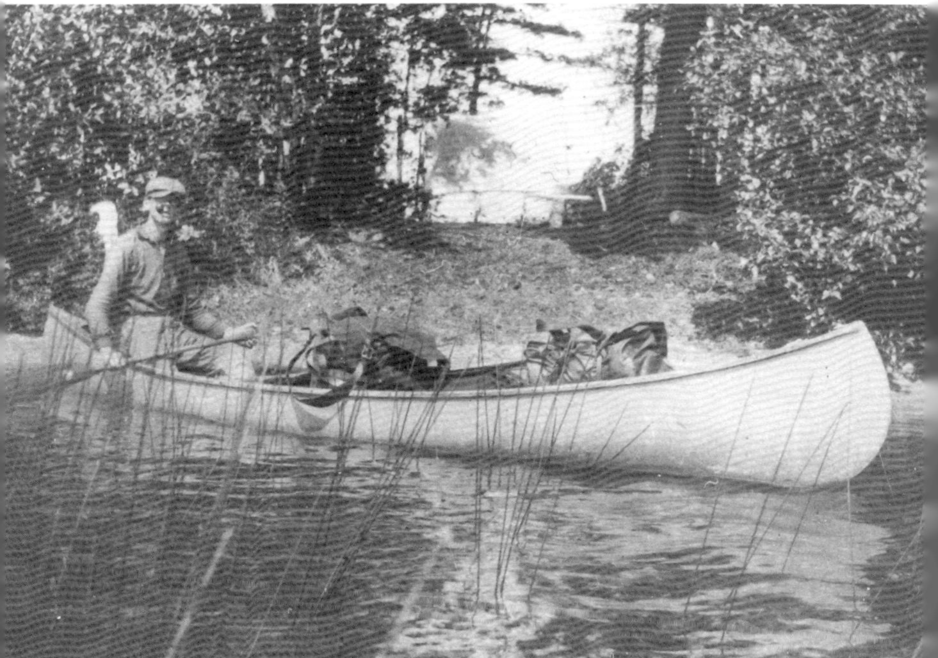

Tom Thomson in a canoe, 1912, Arthur Lismer and Marjorie Lismer Bridges Fonds, Edward P. Taylor Research Library and Archives, Art Gallery of Ontario

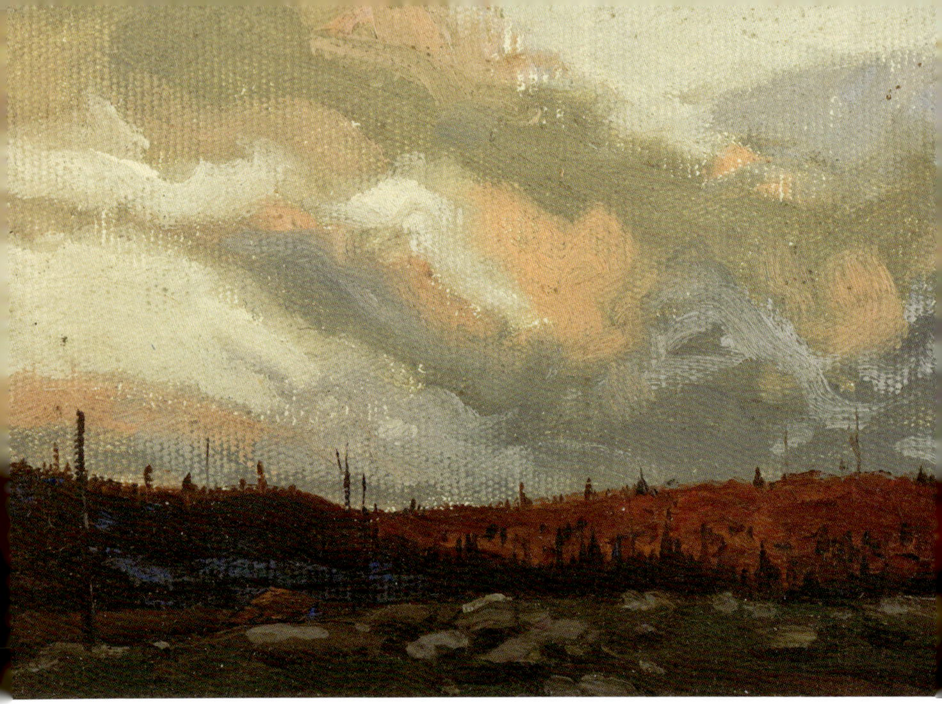

Tom Thomson, *Red Forest*, McMichael Canadian Art Collection

Tom lived on bacon, flapjacks, fish and potatoes. Shannon Fraser, proprietor of Mowat Lodge, called on Tom to guide when George Rowe and Lawrie Dickson were drunk or otherwise on the outs. This year Tom met the Trainors, who owned The Manse, a cottage next to Mowat Lodge on the shore of Canoe Lake—Hugh, Margaret and their adult daughters Winnie and Marie.[167]

Tom dug out his city duds to dance with both young women at Mowat Lodge and Algonquin Hotel on Joe Lake, and dug them out again for dinner at The Manse. Tom McCormack, Marie's future husband, thought Tom a rounder, a drunk and a bum.[168]

In August Tom explored the park's north end—Manitou Lake, North Tea Lake. He sketched sunsets, storms, silhouettes, a spectrum of greys: *Lake, Shore, and Sky*; *Northland*

Sunset; *Canoe Lake*; *Moonlight*; *Morning Cloud;* and ironically, *Red Forest.* There was some colour—the baby blue, pink and lilac of *Evening*; the yellow, orange and pinks of *Sky (The Light That Never Was)*; and the orange, reds and greens of *Autumn, Algonquin Park.*

Tom showed his sketches to Ranger Mark Robinson and the sixteen-year-old sister of Canoe Lake Section man Charlie Ruttan. "Oh!" she gushed, "just like the alders were a week ago."[169] Tom cracked a whimsical grin. Afterwards, Tom turned to Robinson and said, "Why, that's the finest compliment I've ever gotten!"[170]

On his way back to Toronto, Tom stopped in at Huntsville to say "so long" to the Trainors. He thanked them for their hospitality through the summer. He also said goodbye to his friend Doc McRuer, who was ill with TB. McRuer told Tom he was moving to Colorado to take the fresh air cure, the very cure Algonquin was thought to offer. McRuer succumbed to the disease in a scant four years, only days before Tom himself passed away.

Back in Toronto, Tom met with two men who would change his life—Dr. James MacCallum and A.Y. "Alex" Jackson. MacCallum wrote:

> *Autumn came again, and at last my numerous inquiries were rewarded by the information that "Tom has come home again." His hiding place in a boarding house I at last discovered, and found his walls covered with sketches. Half of them I borrowed to look over at my leisure, for he had sought to depict lightning flashes, moving thunderstorms, and trees with branches lashing in the wind. These sketches so interested the painter A.Y. Jackson, that he asked to meet Thomson.*[171]

Jackson had come from Montreal the previous spring to meet J.E.H. MacDonald and Lawren Harris, who purchased Jackson's *The Edge of the Maple Wood* in 1911. Both men had written Jackson, inviting him to join their fledgling school. Feeling "the sacred fires about to burst into flame,"[172] Jackson agreed to stay in Toronto. He spent the summer with family at their Georgian Bay cottage, then at the "modest millionaire's"[173] cottage in nearby Go Home Bay. Dr. MacCallum made Jackson the same offer he had made to MacDonald—to pay his expenses for the year so he could paint full-time.

Tom met Jackson at Harris's studio above the Bank of Commerce at Bloor and Yonge. Despite MacCallum's enthusiasm, Jackson was less impressed with Tom's sketches.

"Sombre, dead in colour. No gay little rapids or wood interiors. No patterned rocks. Only opposite shores, lakes, far hills. Big country."[174]

Tom gifted him *Lake, Shore and Sky*, which Jackson thought the best of the bunch. Though Jackson thought Tom's paintings were no great shakes, he found him a friendly chap and liked him well enough to share a studio that winter in the building MacCallum and Harris were having built in Rosedale Valley. Tom found a room in Frank Gavin's boarding house on Wellesley Street.

After buying a few of Tom's sketches—*View Over a Lake: Shore with Houses*; *Thunderhead*; *Autumn; Algonquin Park*—MacCallum made Tom the same offer he had made the others. Tom refused; worried he'd make a fool of himself[175] but was convinced by Jackson shortly thereafter. So Tom decided to give it a shot, to be a full-time painter, like Jackson, Tom's friends Arthur Lismer and J.E.H. MacDonald and like his brother George. Tom resigned to an understanding Albert Robson.

At Lawren Harris's studio, Tom shadowed Jackson as he painted up his canvas—a snowy hilltop, ragged pines intersecting a cloudy sky, brilliant autumn leaves and the beginnings of a rainbow. Harris and MacDonald called it Mount Ararat, site of the earth's rebirth after the great flood in the Book of Genesis.

Tom's former co-worker and would-be protégé Franklin Carmichael visited Tom at his room in Frank Garvin's boarding house on Wellesley Street,[176] "The room was thick with smoke and there was Tom with his huge canvas. It was a northern scene, a distant line of shore and a vast expanse of grey and soggy sky."[177]

Tom's canvas, *Grey Day in the North* was sunlight on water, a distant line of shore swathed in pure green, a vast expanse of grey and soggy sky.

Carmichael would be leaving shortly to study at Lismer and Varley's *alma mater*, The Academie Royale des Beaux-Arts, the trip to Belgium made possible with the free tuition.

One afternoon J.E.H. MacDonald called Tom, asking him to come up to his Thornhill farmhouse to help him finish illustrations and a cover for a booklet commemorating the soon to be opened Toronto General Hospital.

Stanley Kemp remembered:

> *The year Toronto General Hospital was opened in its present location, J.E.H. MacDonald was doing a sizable free-lance job for the hospital authorities and he had hired me to work all day through a public holiday.*
>
> *After all day on the job it was apparent that to finish there was still an all-night job for two men, with the morrow morning being the deadline. I was anxious to get home to my young wife and children and besides I had to go to work at the shop as usual next morning.*

MacDonald was fortunate to get Tommy Thomson on the telephone and greatly happy that the latter would come directly on the radial railway. I can still see MacDonald and me standing as reception committee, watching the last radial car come down the hill and then up the hill into the village, and then, blessed relief, Tommy Thomson getting off as promised. Three pairs of hands, being pumped like pump handles.[178]

Tom and MacDonald worked through the night as MacDonald's son, Thoreau looked on:

It was in winter, I think in 1912 or 1913, that he first came to our house to help my father with some work in commercial design that they hoped to finish by working all night. I hung around hoping to hear something about the North but can only recollect Tom smiling and quietly working. It is his quiet ways I remember best in thinking of him. [179]

Back in Toronto, Jackson introduced Tom to his family friend, Christine Bertram who fed them and mended their clothes in exchange for sketches.[180]

In December, Jackson's sketches adorned the walls of the Arts and Letters Club alongside MacDonald's and Harris's. The most vehement response to the show was a satirical letter that appeared in *The Toronto Daily Star* by "Peter and I," the *nom de plume* of Arts and Letter Club member H.R. Gadsby. "What's this one?" he asked, "a hob-nailed liver, a Plesiosaur in a fit?"[181] In it the painters are dubbed "The Hot Mush School."

Politics was Gadsby's regular beat, a reflection of how unimportant this show was to the paper. MacDonald replied immediately with a letter to the editor, "You have got my goat, my horse, my ass, and everything else which is mine.

Let us support our distinctly native art, if only for the sake of experiment."[182]

By January, the Studio Building was nearly done. Tom and Jackson moved into Studio One on the ground floor. They joined MacDonald, Lismer and Harris, as well as Art Heming, Curtis Williamson and Bill Beatty, three painters united only in their mutual dislike. Beatty, that glorious truculent bigot,[183] belaboured the workmen at their task.

Tom Thomson and the War

By 1914 Thomson was back on top. Unlike his time in Seattle, he didn't have a serious relationship, or at least not a relationship he was serious about, but he did have a calling in landscape painting; a patron in Dr. James MacCallum, who was paying his bills for the year; a teacher in Alex Jackson, who would help him develop his distinct style; and a support network in the Hot Mush painters.

Thomson still visited his family in Owen Sound, but he also had a family in the painters with whom he lived and worked. Most importantly, he had found his landscape in Algonquin Park. The land William Brodie had told him about. The land to which he belonged.

Tragically, the war threw Thomson's world into disarray. His friends scattered. The tourist trade in Algonquin Park and the design work in Toronto dried up. And government spending on the arts disappeared as well, reallocated to the war effort.[184]

Amazingly Thomson did not cut and run as he had in Seattle. Even without the moral support of his painter friends and the financial support of government purchases, he persevered. He channelled his loneliness, his money worries, even the war itself into his painting.

What he lacked in formal art school learning, he gleaned from his friends or was taught by them. He synthesized their lessons into a unique style that emerged under Jackson's tutelage and flowered during the desolation of war.

Some may see the desolation of war in Thomson's vibrant landscapes,[185] but with Brodie's philosophy in mind you can easily see the exact opposite: Life, not death. Look at Jackson's *A Copse, Evening 1918* or Varley's *German Prisoners.* These are landscape paintings that show the desolation of war. The trees are blasted, the landscape beaten and muddied. Compare Thomson's landscapes during the war years. They are full of life! Vibrant. Vital. A statement by Thomson perhaps, that in the midst of death—Thomson referred to the war as "the machine"[186]—there is still life.

With guidance from his painter friends, Tom learned to paint a landscape that pulls the viewer in. This is accomplished by having a foreground one must look beyond to see the middle ground. Jackson's *Red Maple* used a sapling as a screen, not to keep the viewer out, but to intrigue them, to coyly draw them in. Thomson employed this technique in *Northern River.*

But Thomson began to do something his friends had not taught him. In the background of an increasing number of landscapes, Thomson began to paint a way in, a distant entrance, promising something beyond a purely aesthetic experience.

That discovery hit me like a flash of lightning in the dim quiet of the National Gallery in Ottawa. I saw it in Thomson's masterpiece, *The Jack Pine*, and afterwards I began to find it in his other paintings as well. Could this be the final piece of the puzzle? Was I ready to answer the riddle of the Canadian sphinx at last?

CHAPTER SEVEN

Sky (The Light that Never Was) Tom Finds His Style

The Studio Building

Cupped in Rosedale Valley, north of city limits. A Canadian
echo of its eponymous twin in New York. Next to
the village of Yorkville, half a century away
from its own bohemian occupation.
Eden Smith designed the three-story block. Utilitarian
in comparison with his usual fare—tony mansions for
Toronto's moneyed—but with dormers, hipped roofs,
multi-paned windows to catch the light.
Six double-height studios. Each with a fireplace, cottagey
living-room, wrought-iron stairs leading to a modest
loft. At twenty-two dollars a month, steep
for a struggling artist.

Tom and Jackson painted together in Studio One. Jackson's sparkling, vibrant colour opened Tom's eyes. True doesn't mean photographic. It's personal. It conveys more than just appearance—emotion, meaning, truth. Not so different from design really. Lift it up. Pull it out.[187] Jackson introduced Tom to his heroes—van Gogh, Matisse. "See how Monet loves the air."

Though at first Tom refused to move a branch or change the contour of a hill, he appointed the skies with broken strokes, brightening both *Moonlight* and *Morning Cloud.* Franklin Carmichael described their studio.

> *Three easels stand at the far end of the room. A waste paper basket topped by a palette in front of one. Alongside another, a sketchingstool and a drawing board. The table too is covered with half-used tubes of paint, brushes, a bottle of oil, turpentine, bottles, sketches, and colour boxes. Behind the easels, in great array, canvases and frames, not without disorder.*[188]

Through the winter, Jackson taught Tom how to mix paint, brushwork, colour—Alizarin Crimson, Vermillion Hue, Cadmium Yellow, Cobalt Yellow, Viridian, Ultramarine Blue, Freeman's White. There were lively interchanges of opinion, frank discussions on aims and ideals, on technical problems that resulted in various experiments.[189]

To get more vibrant colours, Lawren Harris dragged his brush quickly through three or four colours and slapped it on the canvas. Among the Hot Mushers, this method was known as Tomato Soup.[190]

Tom also proved a willing pupil for Studio Building tenants Heming, Williamson, and Beatty, who later claimed to have taught him all he knew. Tom built a new sketch box to accommodate the larger sketch boards favoured by Jackson. They ordered their boards from the same Kitchener plant. For dinner they walked to Yonge and Bloor, to The Busy Bee.[191] Some Saturdays they raised the fifteen cents to see a moving picture at The Yorkville—*The Last Days of Pompeii, Bangville Police.*

Tom Thomson, *Morning Cloud,* 1913, The Thomson Collection at Art Gallery of Ontario

Tom joined his Hot Mush colleagues in the Second Exhibition of Little Pictures at the Public Reference Library—*Cumulus Clouds, Evening, Grey Day, Northern Lake, Winter.* None of Tom's sketches sold. But to be invited! To have work worth showing! To be a part of the group.

At the 1914 Ontario Society of Artists exhibition in March, Tom showed *Morning Cloud, Moonlight* and *Early Evening,* the latter was purchased by Eric Brown, new director of the National Gallery. For the first time, Tom was listed as a member of the OSA. Jackson was not so fortunate. His masterpiece, which came to be called *Terre Sauvage,* went unsold.

While Charlie Chaplin waddled and The Toronto Blue Shirts won the Stanley Cup, Jackson journeyed to Algonquin Park. He told MacDonald and Beatty, who joined him there shortly after, "Supply yourself with plenty of madder, blue,

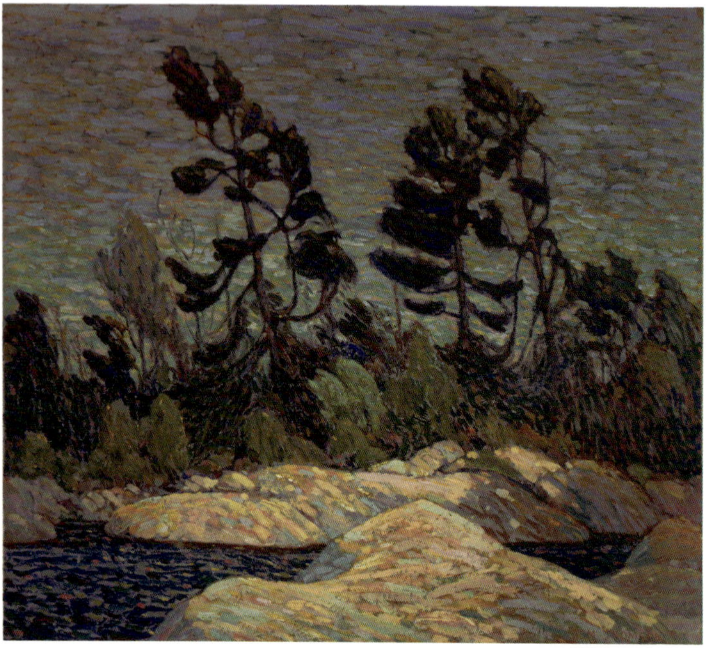
Tom Thomson, *Byng Inlet,* McMichael Canadian Art Collection

and white!"[192] Although all three painters had painted the land of Central Ontario, they considered Algonquin "a revelation," finding objectionable only the collection of comic gramophone records at the lodge.[193] Jackson returned to the studio and painted up *Frozen Lake, Early Spring* and *Algonquin Park* with subtle blues. Violets and mauves shadow snow. Sunlit snow reflects pale yellows, creamy whites.

Froze hard last night, lake iced over, this morning. I went across portage to Canoe L. only to find the ice had not started out yet. Came back, & went up river in aft. & up along shore to P.O. got a lot of mail & posted some. Lower end of Lake full of ice. Saw Tom Thompson [sic] (artist).[194]

–Journal of Bud Callighen, Friday May 1, 1914

Arthur Lismer joined Tom at the park that spring. Like Beatty, MacDonald and Jackson, he found the park a revelation. They canoed and camped—Canoe Lake, Smoke Lake, Ragged Lake, Crown Lake. Lismer was amazed at Tom's facility in the bush. "He saw a thousand things—animals and birds—and signs along the trail that others missed."[195]

Tom was not happy camping unless he did three-quarters of the work. Paddling, setting up camp, cooking, cleaning up, breaking camp, paddling. He enjoyed playing host, guide to "The Bronc," revealing a world heretofore unseen, unimagined. Lismer sketched like an impressionist, captured changing effects of the light, careless of detail. Tom's sketches became freer, broader.

With *Hoar Frost*, Tom made a negative of the scene—white sky, white trees, snow-covered bushes against white hills, opposed by dark green turf, dark pines that bite into the sky. Red soil peeks out from the turf, elbows through a worn jersey.

After Lismer left, Tom painted his way to Dr. MacCallum's cottage—*Parry Sound Harbour, Spring, French River, Byng Inlet, Georgian Bay, Evening, Pine Island.*

Tom met with Dr. McCallum, and the two canoed and camped together. One raining morning, Tom spins a yarn:

> *I had been sketching in the park and made up my mind to go farther in, two days' journey. So I decided to lighten my load by leaving my sketches to dry, and to pick them up on my way back. On my return I found that a lynx had come along and after a critical inspection of one of my sketches, had clawed it. Not satisfied with this expression of opinion, he had put his head down and chewed it.*
>
> *I am only a bum artist anyway. Why, even the animals know that!*[196]

Tom gave the doctor's daughter painting lessons, gifted her a sketch: *Boathouse, Go Home Bay.*[197] By July, Tom was ready to leave, writing to Jackson:

> *I am leaving here about the end of the week and back to the woods for the summer.*
>
> *Am sorry I did not take your advice and stick to camping. This place is getting too much like north Rosedale to suit me—all birthday cakes and water ice etc.*[198]

Too tamed by tourists with money.

On his way back to Algonquin Park Tom met musician Ernest Freure. For five days they canoed and camped together. Tom thought, just as "...imperfect notes destroy the soul of music so does imperfect colour destroy the soul of the canvas."[199]

Back at the park, guide George Rowe, remarked, "Tom you are a painter, my cabin could sure use a coat." So, Tom painted Rowe's cabin. Tom also did some guiding. A group of Americans ignored Tom completely as he set up camp, cooked dinner, cleaned up afterwards. In the morning, deep in the bush, they woke up alone.

While the plague-ridden Panama Canal opened and Archduke Franz Ferdinand was shot, the benighted 20th century had its bloody birth, and Tom Thomson turned thirty-seven.

Bad news travelled with the trains. Thousands of British soldiers died in suicide trenches, deadly gas attacks, death from above. Tom had a lean summer for boards. He wrote Fred Varley, "Have not made any sketches for a few weeks but feel like starting again."[200]

Caught 5 small trout this morning, "pearl wobbler" & came back to Smoke L. T. Thompson & A.Y. Jackson here tonight, camped on Windy Point. Very hot today and strong S.W. wind Met large party on Porcupine going to Rock Lake. 5 people with 13 guides.[201]

–Bud Callighen Personal Diary, Monday, September 21

Jackson, returned from an excursion with Bill Beatty—painting the Rockies on the railway's nickel—and rejoined Tom at the park, having found "mountains were not in my line."[202] The two set up base below Tea Lake Dam and travelled through the southwest corner of the park. Tom canoed while Jackson hunted for *motifs* from the prow. They ate good husky meals: bannock, flapjacks, fish, endless kettles of tea. They painted the war news away, the fools who "damn the *Germs* and thereby think they do some good."

Tom struggled to produce. His hand as inarticulate as a hunk of wood. Not only was he unable to capture the scene, what he did create wasn't any good. Shades of Don Valley years before. He hurled his sketch box into the bush. It was retrieved by Jackson and repaired by Bud Callighen the next day.[203]

Although Tom complained, Jackson marveled at his growth:

> *Tom is doing some exciting stuff. He keeps one up to time. Very often I have to figure out if I am leading or following. You need a man who tries to do the impossible. To do what you know is easily within your powers never has given rise to a great school of art or anything else. I can finish up the autumn sketching and still be in plenty of time to fight the Germs. There are sure to be some of them left.*[204]

***Picture this:** Tom paints in thick strokes left undisturbed, frozen motion. Sunlight glistens on the drying paint, reflections like restless water. Jackson takes Tom to task for giving away his boards so freely. "Alex, it's painting, not the painting that's important." The doing, not the having.*

Fred Varley, Arthur Lismer and their families arrived in October, amazed by the drama of fall. An exercise in relativity—the passengers having aged only eight hours during their train trip from Toronto, while the fall colours were two weeks ahead. Joining them was the painter Beatrice Robertson née Hagerty. Capturing the fall colours in Algonquin was not only a man's game.

***Picture this:** Tom, Jackson, Lismer and Varley surround Larry Dickson's shack. Laptop sketching in broken colour, channelling light, four windows onto the same scene. Lismer scatters pure yellow and orange leaves over a brilliant blue sky. Tom raises his thumb in closed fist, jerks it at him in approval. Varley, unrepentant portraitist, paints his wife, Maud, in the midst of the birch grove.*

Tom made a less successful sketch than his spring version—brilliant blue skies, sunny green branches glimmering over dark green conifers, snow laden branches laid over top.

Discharged from duty, the old Gilmour Mill hospital building housed dozens of drying sketches, propped against abandoned walls.

During their painting expedition, Lismer pulled Tom aside. He dutifully tried to convey the "concerns" Dr. MacCallum had entrusted to him. Tom's angry retort: "Yes, I know what it is. 'You tell Thomson not to let that fellow Jackson influence him.'"[205]

Making no mention of MacCallum's advice or his reaction to it, Tom writes his benefactor:

> *Dear Dr. MacCallum:*
>
> *Jackson has written Harris (who has my Bank Book) to find out my bank balance—I have probably used most of it up by this time and it is just to find out if I should ride or walk back to Toronto.*
>
> *Could you phone the bank and find out?*[206]

Despite Tom's money worries, he abandoned the idea of applying to be a park ranger because of all the red tape. Tom's aversion to (or fear of) bureaucracy would cost him on more than one occasion.

Back in Toronto, bachelors Tom and Jackson feel the wartime mood acutely. Recruiting sergeants call from every corner, "Sign up now, or you'll miss it." Bitterly, Tom muttered, "Six months, hell. Three or four years. It must be."[207]

Jackson was in no desperate hurry to enlist either, "There are lots of institutions and big fat heads in this country not worth laying down one's life to preserve. They should send the politicians to the front."[208]

MacCallum strolled over from his Bloor Street office to the painters' studio teasing, "You can't tell me you ever saw anything like that!"

"You fellows must have something wrong with your eyesight," he said. Then just before he left, he added, "Well, I think I'll take this along with me." And he dug into his pocket for some bills. [209]

Jackson painted up *Red Maple,* dashed crimson leaves against a dark blue brook to create depth, whisked white to set the water in motion. He explained to Tom as he went.

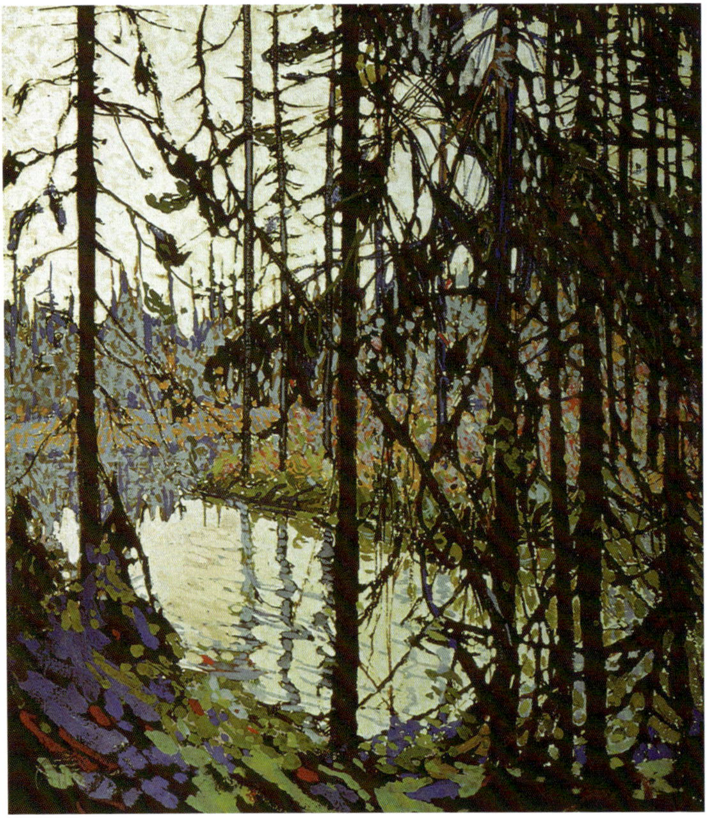

Tom Thomson, Study for *"Northern River,"* 1914–1915, The Thomson Collection at Art Gallery of Ontario

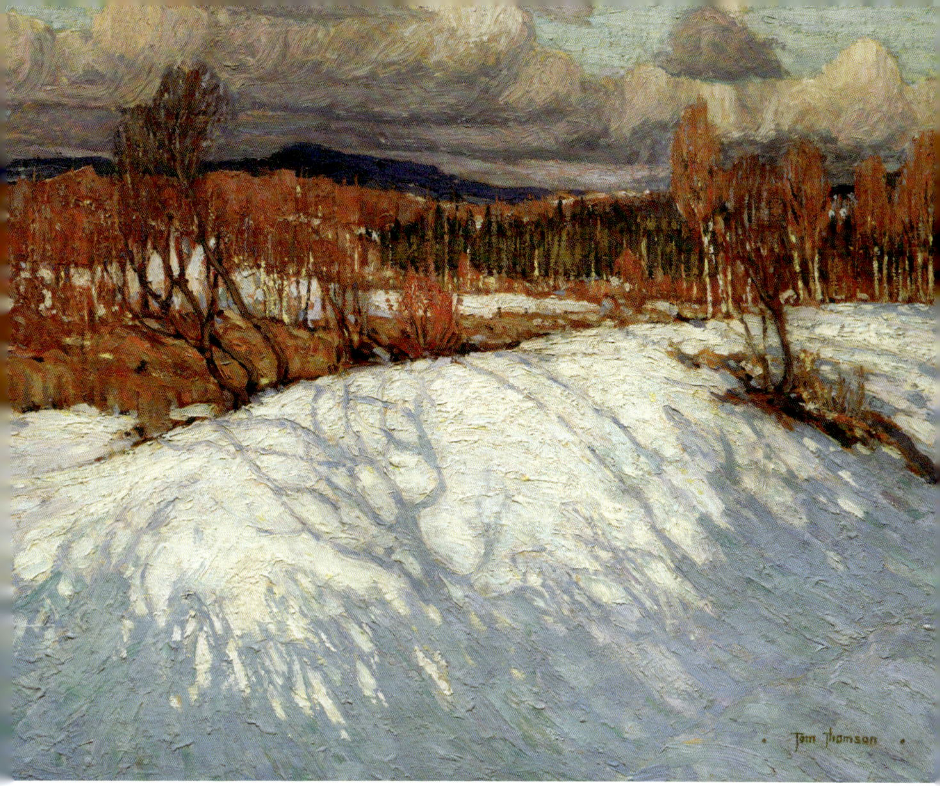

Tom Thomson, *In Algonquin Park*, McMichael Canadian Art Collection

Rather than working from a sketch, Tom painted up a study for *Northern River* in the studio. He used gouache instead of oils, stretching pure blue, red, green across a forest bed of black, latticing the foreground with silhouette trees. Dead trees reflected from the far shore reiterated by river, sky palely loitering.

He painted up a canvas for *Petawawa Gorges* (*Early Spring*). Warmed it up with pinks and baby blues, set the horizontal strokes of lake, sky, against the vertical stroke of the far shore. He introduced lumber to the canvas for *In Algonquin Park*, adding drama to the clouds. Like Jackson's *Maple Wood*, he dragged shadows across the canvas from behind the viewer, spectral fingers pointing to the twisted trees. At Jackson's urging, he added his own shadow among the trees, becoming a part of the painting, not apart from it.

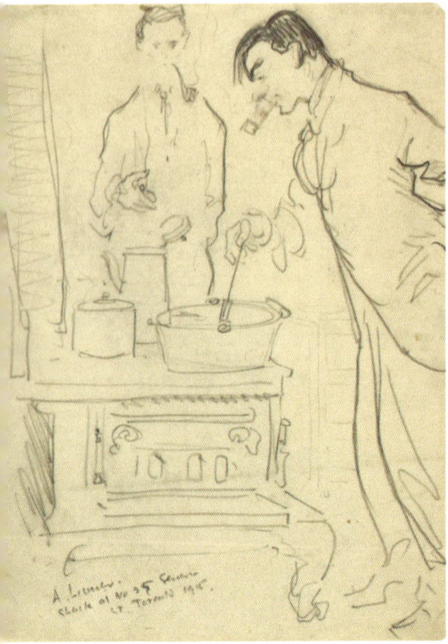

Arthur Lismer, *Shack at No. 25 Severn Street Toronto,* 1915, National Gallery of Canada

In November, Tom showed his work for the first time at the Royal Canadian Academy show held at the Public Library on Church Street: *A Lake, Early Spring, Frost After Rain. In Algonquin Park* was sold at a special sale for The Patriotic Fund war effort, $50 to Marion Long, a new tenant at the Studio Building and founder of The Heliconian Club (where Tom would have a solo show).

That winter, Tom got a commission to design tourism posters for Owen Sound—*Industrial Center/Summer Resort!* Despite the work, Tom's circumstances were straitened. He tightened his belt even further.

A changing of the guard, Tom's former co-worker Franklin Carmichael returned from art school in Europe just as Jackson returned to Montreal, his year of patronage from Dr. MacCallum having ended. Carmichael and Tom agreed to share a studio for the winter. Christmas came. The war did not end, showed no sign of slowing down—pan-oceanic best wishes, absent fathers, lovers, sons.

Tom visited the MacDonalds in their Thornhill home, a member of the family. One Sunday dinner at the Lismers' on Delaware Avenue, Fred Varley acts up. Carmichael wrote his girlfriend, Ada Went:

Sunday evening, Tom and I went up to Arthur's [with] *Mrs. Varley and Fred. It was not quite as enjoyable an evening as I have spent there before. Through no fault of ours, or Arthur's, Fred is again showing a side of his nature, which does not always make for sociability.*

It only needed a few words to cap the whole thing, which were spoken by Fred, not more than two minutes after we arrived. I have never seen Tom so angry, or have I been ever so put out, as on Sunday evening.

It is rotten, and I feel as if I want to chuck Fred entirely, as one never knows when one is going to be subjected to a process of freezing which is anything but pleasant. So for my own part I hope he doesn't put in an appearance around here until he has learned to control his temper and his mind and all that. Enough of this, it makes me a bit miserable to think about it.[210]

The Hot Mushers lived and worked in the Studio Building. The artists shared canvases, painted and traded advice about each other's work. Tom and Carmichael's studio became a centre of gravity, a congregating place.

Carmichael wrote his girlfriend:

You said you would like to be a concealed onlooker when Tom and I were preparing our meals. I too wish you could, as no doubt you would see some queer sights, and when a finger is burnt or some stuff boiled over, overhear remarks not heard everyday in a kitchen. The rest of the fellows are all glad to come in and have a snack. That speaks well for our cooking doesn't it? We really have an enjoyable time as we visit, gabbing away like so many geese.[211]

Everyone contributed his particular talent: Irish stew, Mulligan. Bill Beatty fried potatoes, made oyster stew.

Dr. MacCallum, "patron saint" of the Studio Building, "Comes in, flops down in a chair, throws matches on the floor and talks in an intelligent way about our work, taking as keen an interest as one's self."[212]

He set the painters up with freelance work when he could, tasked Carmichael with anatomical diagrams of the eye.[213]

Dr. MacCallum took Tom, Carmichael and fellow Studio Building tenant, Arthur Heming to a boxing match at Broadview and King.[214]

Champion Tommy Tootel of Riversides beats the hard-hitting Red Gallagher to the punch every time. Finally, in the second round, knocks him through the ropes with a heavy right swing. Gallagher gamely climbs back in and rushes Tootel, who coolly drops him again. Referee Hewitt gives him a minute to come to and he weathers the round, but two punches finish the job in the third round. Gallagher's head hits the floor with a bump that could be heard all over the arena.[215]

At the Ontario Society of Arts show in March 1915, Tom's *Split Rock, Georgian Bay, Pines,* and *A Northern River* were lauded in an article that listed George Thomson as "Mr. Tom Thomson's brother." The latter canvas was purchased by the National Gallery of Canada for $500.

Mail and Empire, March 13, 1915

There are 187 pictures in the gallery, representing the work of about 70 artists and the paintings cover a very wide range, both in subject and method of treatment. There are some canvases of the old school, which dominated all our exhibitions a few years ago, tranquil little landscapes painted in a pleasant manner. Then, in marked contrast, stands out the work of the younger men, whose radical ideas have undoubtedly put a new vitality into Canadian art.

A large and arresting canvas by Mr. Tom Thomson is *Northern River*. One of the most striking pictures of its kind and bears close examination. Its striking colour holds the attention first, but beyond that tangled foreground is a destination of very real beauty.[216]

Tom left Toronto earlier than ever, travelling first to Owen Sound, then Huntsville to stock up. There he painted Winnie Trainor into *Snow in the Village*, one of several paintings to feature people this year. Tom would never be a figure man like Lismer or a portraitist like Varley. Instead, Tom painted portraits of trees bent by wind, bowed by snow but standing still, surviving. Tom's friend Lawren Harris understood what Tom saw in the trees. In his poem, "Old Pine," Harris wrote, "Moan over and over again/ I am beautiful because I struggle."[217]

Back in Algonquin, Tom went up the track behind the section house to the old dam on Potter Creek. He painted the ice breaking up—blustery blues and greens, rotten ice screened by branches, grey and brown. Then he hiked back to the station, stamped his feet to thaw out as he waited for postmaster and proprietor of Mowat Lodge, Shannon Fraser to come for the mail.

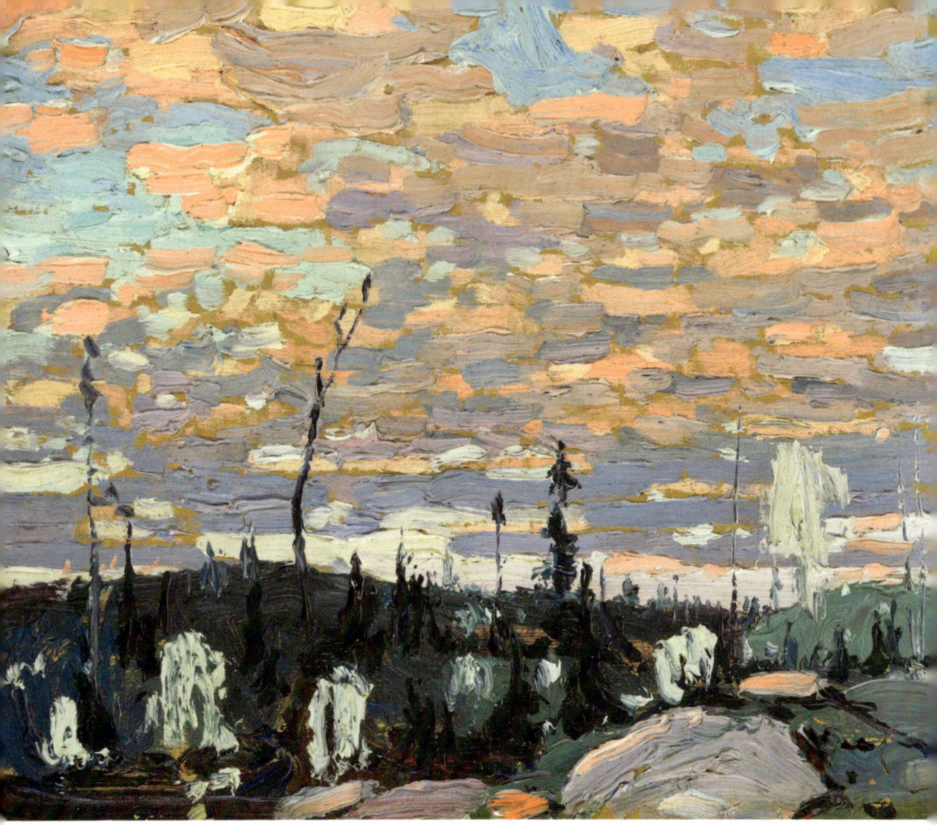

Tom Thomson, *Wild Cherries, Spring,* McMichael Canadian Art Collection

By the end of April, Tom had already made dozens of sketches: *Burnt Land, Fraser's Lodge, Northern Spring, Wild Cherries, Spring* and *In the Sugar Bush*, which features Shannon Fraser. Once it was warm enough to camp, Tom left the lodge and set up camp on Hayhurst Point.

> *Paddled up to Mink L. & picked up my box-traps. Met Vanclief (guide) on Tea L. Had come up river from L. of Bay's. Also met Rowe & Thompson with two Johnston boys, (tourists). Very strong west wind, thunder no rain.*[218]
>
> –Bud Callighen Diary, April 28, 1915

The war had effectively killed tourism that summer. Owing to the lack of work—there were sometimes more guides than tourists—Rowe and Tom paired up, half a wage being better than none.

Carmichael wrote his fiancé:

> *Along with your most welcome letter came one from Tom Thomson, extending his congratulations to us, as well as doing a little moralizing on his own account about a bachelor's life. He gave me the benefit of what seems to be his own personal experience and if I read between the lines correctly, it is not untinged with a certain bitterness towards those who claim it is the ideal existence for an artist.*
>
> *Poor old boy, the whole tone of his letter seemed so blue. I wanted to rush up to the park just to have a chat with him and cheer him up a bit. He has these streaks occasionally.*[219]

Tom battled the blues after a letter from Carmichael announcing his betrothal. He thinks:

> *I should be unreservedly happy for Frank and Ada, but instead I write a moralistic letter decrying the state of celibacy which some claim is ideal for artists. Ha! Most every man needs love, needs the support only a good wife can provide. It's not that I don't want a wife, it's that I'm not fit for one. Too wild, too moody, too irresponsible. Sure Arthur and Mr. MacDonald can manage a family, though they suffer greatly for it. But I am too much like Fred, although I hate to admit it. Unlike him, I will not impose myself and my life on a woman and children as well.*

Tom was restless.

I have made quite a few sketches this summer but lately have not been doing much and have a notion of starting out on a long hike and will likely wind up somewhere around the French River and go up the shore to Bruce Mines and later on may take in the Harvest Excursion and work at the wheat for a month or two.[220]

Instead, Tom painted the park, capturing enormous summer skies, clouds like zeppelins, dreadnoughts, floating passively overhead, beautiful bloody sunsets owing to the eruption of Lassen Peak in California that past May.

After the disastrous second battle of Ypres in June, it was clear to all that the war would not be over by that Christmas, nor perhaps the next. In Montreal, Tom's friend and future Group of Seven member A.Y. Jackson enlisted, refusing offers of a commission: "I knew nothing about soldiering, and decided to start at the bottom, as a private in the infantry."[221]

When he heard about Jackson, Tom wrote MacDonald, deeply dismayed:

As with yourself, I can't get used to the idea of Jackson being in the machine, and it is rotten that in this so called civilized age that such things can exist, but since this war has started it will have to go on until our side wins out, and of course there is no doubt which side it will be, and we will see Jackson back on the job once more.[222]

On July 27 in Algonquin Park, a local boy, Alex Hayhurst, was laid to rest in the makeshift cemetery that would one day hold Tom's remains. Diphtheria. Park Ranger Bud Callighen took Mr. Munger out to read the service:

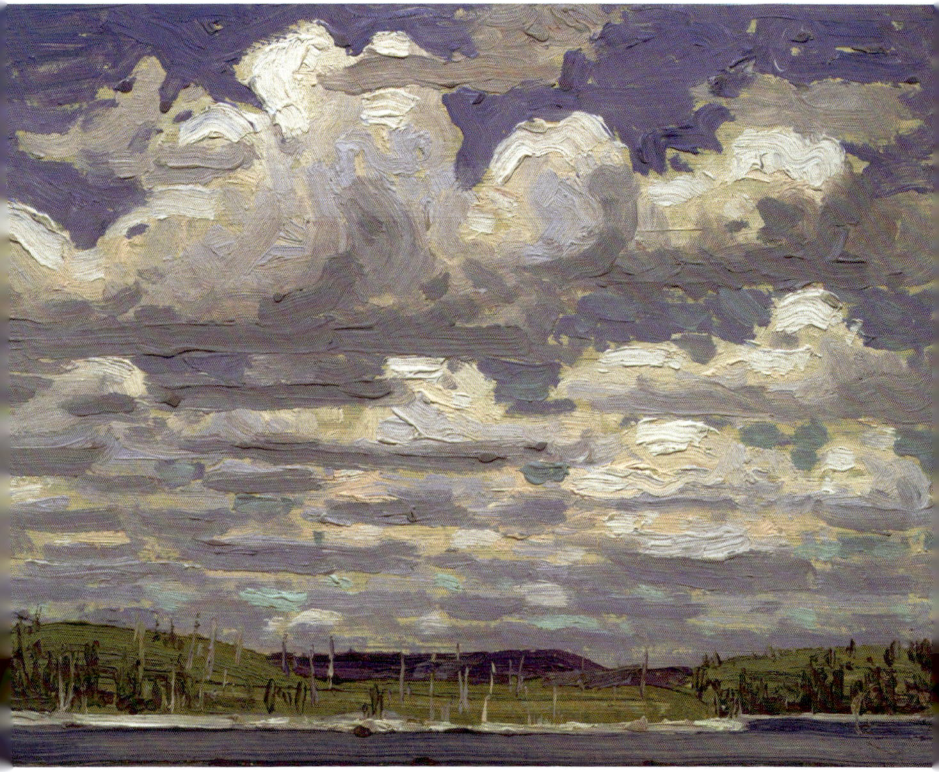

Tom Thomson, *Summer Day,* McMichael Canadian Art Collection

As a father is tender toward his children, so is the Lord tender to those who fear him. For he knows of what we are made; he remembers that we are but dust, our days are like grass; we flourish like a flower of the field; when the wind goes over it, it is gone and its place will know it no more.[223]

We brought nothing into this world, and we take nothing away. The Lord giveth and the Lord taketh away; blessed be the name of the Lord.[224]

In August 1915, more than 100,000 people gathered in Toronto's Riverdale Park to watch fireworks and hear marching bands drum up enthusiasm for the fight. Two spirited young ladies made their way through the crowd, joyously bestowing white chicken feathers on th astonished and outraged young men standing around.[225]

Up at the park, Tom canoed up to the Magnetawan River. He sketched the running of the logs, swirling a frothy pink sky over a pyramid of *Abandoned Logs*, shattered on a choppy lake. Up by South River, Thomson tramped 14 miles carrying a sketch box and a gun; there he bagged, seven partridges and a sketch of Sand Hill.[226] He picked up his mail, and stocked up on supplies, and boards from the veneer mill. At Ard's store Tom treated himself to a baloney sandwich, biscuits and a bottle of pop.[227]

For the first time, Tom's paintings were shown at the Canadian National Exhibition in The Gallery of Fine Arts. *In Georgian Bay, Pines, Georgian Bay* sat beside the work of established Canadian artists such as Horatio Walker and Homer Watson, who Oscar Wilde had dubbed, "the Canadian Constable."

The Ex had a distinctly patriotic flavour that year: a model military camp with trenches, all kinds of engines and implements of destruction, a "Remarkable Exhibit of War Trophies including a captured Krupp gun and a blood-stained cap of a Teuton," and, of course, a recruiting booth.

Back at Canoe Lake, ranger Mark Robinson grew used to seeing Tom idly tossing stones in the Joe Creek rapids, tearing around looking for a scene. Tom ran up to Robinson's cabin:

"Say Mark you know. I know you know."

"Tom just tell me what you want and possibly I can help you."

"Three trees. Spruce trees, black spruce rough old looking trees. You know what I mean. Where can I get them, at once?"

"Go to the little wharf below Sim's Pit you will find those trees you want in a grove." He was away like a shot. Robinson's wife asked, "Is he slightly…demented?"[228]

Three days later Tom was back, a smile on his face, and *Black Spruce In Autumn* in hand. "Say Mark, those trees were just what I required, and the sky was just right. How do you always know what I want?"[229]

Tom, who was 38, tried to enlist but was rejected[230] as he was in ninety-nine, for fallen arches. Robinson, at 47 years of age,[231] was called up that fall.

Tom had asked Carmichael up to Algonquin, but he was otherwise occupied with his wedding. As a gift:

> *Tom gave instructions to wander around to his shack and select anything in the way of "wall decorations" we wished and as many as we wished. It may sound hoggish, but I have such deep admiration for his work, I would like to clear the place out. But that would not do, so I shall say we shall be very happy with one or maybe two and these we shall value, always.*[232]

After the wedding, Carmichael left The Studio Building, Toronto, and full-time painting behind, to move to the nearby community of Bolton with his bride.

Although he is sometimes accused of profligacy, Tom worried often about his lack of money. When *Northern River* was finally purchased by the National Gallery, Tom wrote to MacCallum to enquire about the money:

> *I sent a check down to the Bank at Bloor and Yonge which would arrive there Sat. morning and so far have not heard from it (and) so conclude that my account has gone broke. It was for $25.00 for stocking up, could you see Harris and get the amount from him and have it sent to me here as I am stranded. I may possibly hear from the Bank today but have almost given up hope.*[233]

Public funds were redirected into the war effort. The National Gallery cut its budget by 75 percent, the Royal Canadian Academy by half. The Ontario government stopped buying art entirely, stopped funding the OSA.

Tom's solitary productivity continued into the fall. *Golden Autumn* was staccato jabs of orange, mustard yellow, counterpoints of deep blue, violet, and aqua. The sunset broiled pink clouds. Skies were an impossible colour between yellow, blue and green.

In November, Tom was in Round Lake. He stayed with park ranger Tom Wattie and his family, square danced at South River. Before heading back to Canoe Lake he lightened his load by firing some of his less successful sketches. The multi-coloured flames delighted Wattie's young children.[234]

From the park, Tom travelled to Owen Sound, arriving after midnight to be met by his aunt Henrietta and Tom's sister Minnie who was visiting from her home in Saskatchewan for the first time in eight years.

Minnie wrote:

> *I noticed a great change in Tom. He seemed engrossed with his work and much quieter. He told us then that he was going to try again to enlist, and if they turned him down he might come west and paint the Rocky Mountains. He was worried too that no one was buying pictures. However in the spring the call of the north was too strong to resist and we were disappointed again.*[235]

Distance makes the heart more perceptive to the increments of personal growth too subtle to be seen day-to-day. Strength, confidence, clarity of vision can look like remoteness, reticence.

When Tom returned to Toronto, it was to the shack behind the Studio Building. The twenty-two-dollar-a-month rent on a studio had become unaffordable. He paid a token one dollar a month for the shack and shared it during the day with Arthur Lismer. Lismer and his family, in likewise precarious circumstances, had moved in with the MacDonalds, who were trying to make a go of their Thornhill farm.

Harris, Lismer and MacDonald all praised Tom's sketches, but not overly as it only seemed to embarrass him. Harris in particular was dazzled by Tom's use of colour. *Black Spruce and Maple* went through him like a spear.

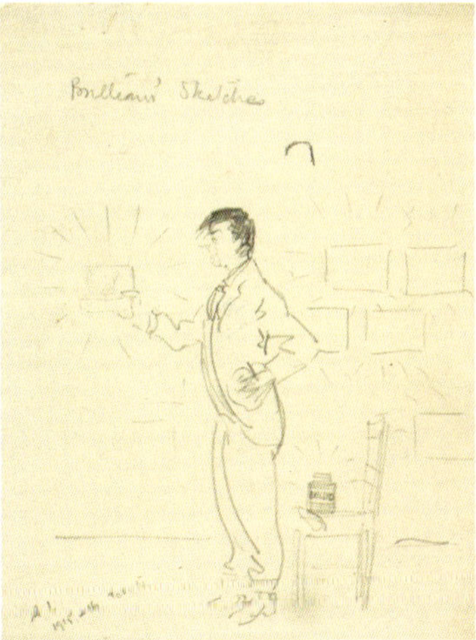

Arthur Lismer, *Brilliant sketches,* National Gallery of Canada

"I'll buy this one Tom, also the rapid sketch, and you must paint up *Burnt Land*."[236]

MacDonald was taken with Tom's flower studies, *Marguerites, Wood Lilies and Vetch*, and *Water Flowers*—delicate yet vital, vibrantly set against an inky black background.[237]

Tom Paints a Passage

I have to admit, I'm pretty nervous now that it comes down to it. I'm not an art historian, not an art critic, but here I am challenging the ideas of one of Canada's foremost thinkers. What will the Thomson experts think, the ones I've admired and referenced in my book? Will they think I'm tilting at windmills rather than riddling with sphinxes?

Thomson was surviving the stress, and the straitened circumstances of the war. He had found the landscape that resonated with him, the landscape in which he felt an integral part. And he was continuing to develop his own style, building on the techniques of his fellow Hot Mushers.

He was putting William Brodie's philosophy into practice, using his paintings to "construct intelligence out of nature, nature out of intelligence and demonstrate the harmony between the two." Thomson's paintings were inspired by the landscape, and the landscapes came to life in his paintings. Tom's painter friends and several art critics who reviewed his works experienced that harmony. The Ruttan girl[238] certainly experienced it.

It is a sense of the vitality of nature. But there was something more, Thomson had found a way to invite the viewer in to his landscapes. A way that could help them to see themselves as an integral part of nature.

From about 1916 you can begin to see a pattern in Thomson's paintings. Look past the foreground that intrigues the viewer, draws them coyly in. Past also the midground rivers and lakes. In the background, on the distant shores, he begins to paint a pathway, a way in.

Half a lifetime after I first felt the dissonance of the traditional interpretation of Thomson's works, I had an alternative. Thomson wasn't painting an unvisualized land with a sinister something concealed within. He was painting an invitation to a vital, vibrant landscape, a place we belong.

This is what I saw in *The Jack Pine* and subsequently found in *The West Wind, In The Northland, Petawawa Gorges, After The Sleet Storm* and several others. For me, this was the final piece of the puzzle. Thomson, consciously or unconsciously, put a pathway into his paintings. An invitation to the viewer, not just to become a part of the scene, but to go beyond the landscape, through it, to become a part of nature.

Here's the complete argument:

1. Thomson's elderly cousin and self-taught naturalist William Brodie told him about his post-Darwin philosophy, about how art could connect people with nature, could confirm our place as an integral part of nature.

2. Thomson painted the Algonquin landscape because he felt connected to it as Brodie had before him.

3. Thomson, consciously or unconsciously, painted a pathway into many of his later paintings not only to draw viewers into his landscapes but also to invite them to enter nature itself, to take their place as an integral part of nature.

Could this be the answer to the Canadian sphinx? The rebuttal to Frye's interpretation of Thomson's work? Or, will the Canadian sphinx tear me to bits, scattering my bones in the wilderness as Frye wrote it did to Thomson? I began to assemble my argument, to integrate it into my stylized biography.

It was in the final years of Thomson's career, of his life, that he created his "pathway" paintings. He spent more of his time up in the park in those years and had even fewer painter friends around him because of the war.

In the absence of supportive painter friends and under increasingly difficult financial constraints—we know Thomson often worried about money—it must have been difficult for Thomson to stick with painting. Although he had run away from difficulties in the past—his apprenticeship in Owen Sound and his life in Seattle—he didn't stop painting. In fact, his production during this time was prodigious, and the quality was the best of his career.

The idea of running away must have crossed Thomson's mind though. He wrote his father in 1917:

> *I did not send any paintings to the O.S.A. Exhibition this year and have not sold very many sketches but think I can manage to get along for another year at least I will stick to painting as long as I can.*[239]

But he didn't run away. Instead he did something few painters had ever accomplished. He made a painting a day for 62 days straight, a daily record of the weather for what was to be the last spring of his life.[240] Instead of leaving, he embraced both painting and the landscape—the daily weather!—even more deeply.

This record is also redolent of William Brodie's influence. Brodie told his protégé, naturalist Ernest Thompson Seton, to keep a journal of his travels: "you will value it more each year."[241] As Joan Murray posited in *Tom Thomson: Design for a Canadian Hero*, Tom likely received the same advice from Brodie and was putting it into action.

So if you're still with me, we have in Tom's paintings not an inhuman sinister something, but an invitation to be a part of vibrant, vital nature. The sphinx has her answer, but the strokes on his paintings, the facts of Tom's life, remain unchanged. This final chapter begins in a refurbished hut in Toronto's Rosedale ravine.

CHAPTER EIGHT

Sunset
The Earth Takes Him Back to Itself

The Shack

In its previous life a chicken coop, a tool shack,
a cabinetmaker's workshop. The shambling shack behind
the Studio Building. Harris and MacCallum resurrect, reroof,
restore, insulate with beaverboard, furnish
with bunk and box stove.
It is a financial expediency, but it also creates a continuity
with Algonquin lodges, ranger's cabins, guide's shacks.

Lures and trolling spoons, axe handles, paddles and snowshoes lined the shack's unpainted walls. A naked bulb hung from the ceiling, stowed behind a fog of tobacco, wood smoke, steam from the kettle and breath when the temperature dipped. J.E.H. MacDonald's son Thoreau wrote:

> *He had a bunk and a little cast-iron range for heat and cooking: the shack was clean and tidy.*
>
> *This had been a little woodworking shop and it was repaired and lined with beaverboard, that forerunner of all modern wallboards. Tom lived and worked there winters until his death in 1917. Some unfinished picture usually stood on the easel and against the wall leaned, at various*

times: The West Wind, The Jack Pine, The Pointers *and other less famous paintings.*

I was more interested in the canoe paddles and axe handles that Tom worked on in intervals of painting and some homemade trolling spoons and lures hanging on the wall. He made and carved his frames too. Seeing my interest in the axe handles he very characteristically gave me a couple and I have one of them still. If you admired his work at all, he was likely to give it to you.[242]

Tom leapt into the air, clasped the bulb's chain between his stocking feet and pulled it down, snapping the light on and somehow landing on his feet. A silent laugh. The bulb's chain swished like a cat's cautionary tail.

In the winter of 1915, the patron saint of the Studio Building struck again. Tom, MacDonald and Lismer painted up panels for MacCallum's cottage. Lismer and MacDonald painted Tom into the mural: a fisherman seated, leg outstretched, a pipe clamped in his teeth, a lumberjack standing, eyes downcast, an insubordinate fist at his hip.

Tom traced the day, the year, through four square panels. He began with a spring nocturne, clumping leaves coolly in gradients of blue and green overtop spectral skies. On the second panel, he scattered brilliant orange leaves against nascent skies of robin's egg blue. The following two: piebald birches with mellow fall foliage in evening, and midday.

Tom's former Gripmate Frank Johnston returned to Toronto after having studied and worked in the United States for several years. Johnston was a frequent visitor to the shack, a larger than life presence, never shy with opinion or advice. Tom had supper with the Johnstons in their York Mills home.

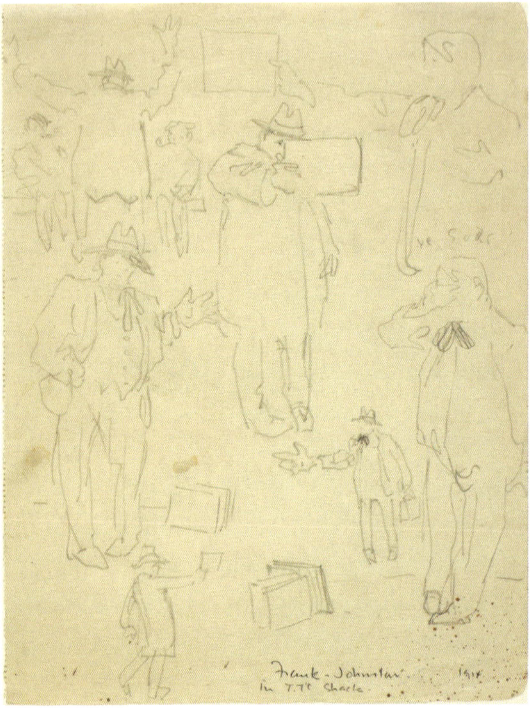

Arthur Lismer, *Frank Johnston in TT's shack,* National Gallery of Canada

The Hot Mushers teased Tom about the scarcity of summer pictures. "Too hot to paint was it? Distracted by the fishes I'll wager. Did you run out of greens?" Tom agreed readily to all suggestions, but the truth was more complicated. It was true that he was busier guiding in the summer, that the browns and greens are less appealing than the colours of fall, but there was something about the change from winter to spring, from fall to winter, the pivot point between seasons, the becoming.

Ensconced in the shack, behind his canvas, Lismer bobbed his gangly head in time to the Victrola:

Stretch your lovin' arms straight out in space
Then do the Eagle Rock with style and grace
Swing your foot way 'round then bring it back,
Now that's what I call Ballin' the Jack.[243]

The canvases Tom painted that winter were delicate, nuanced, compared to the staccato energy of his sketches. The colours less contrasting. The shapes softer. Tom looped gracile trunks over curlicues of birch, ghostly against an azure lake face, a robin's egg blue sky and the premonitory

Tom Thomson, *In The Northland,* Montreal Museum of Fine Arts

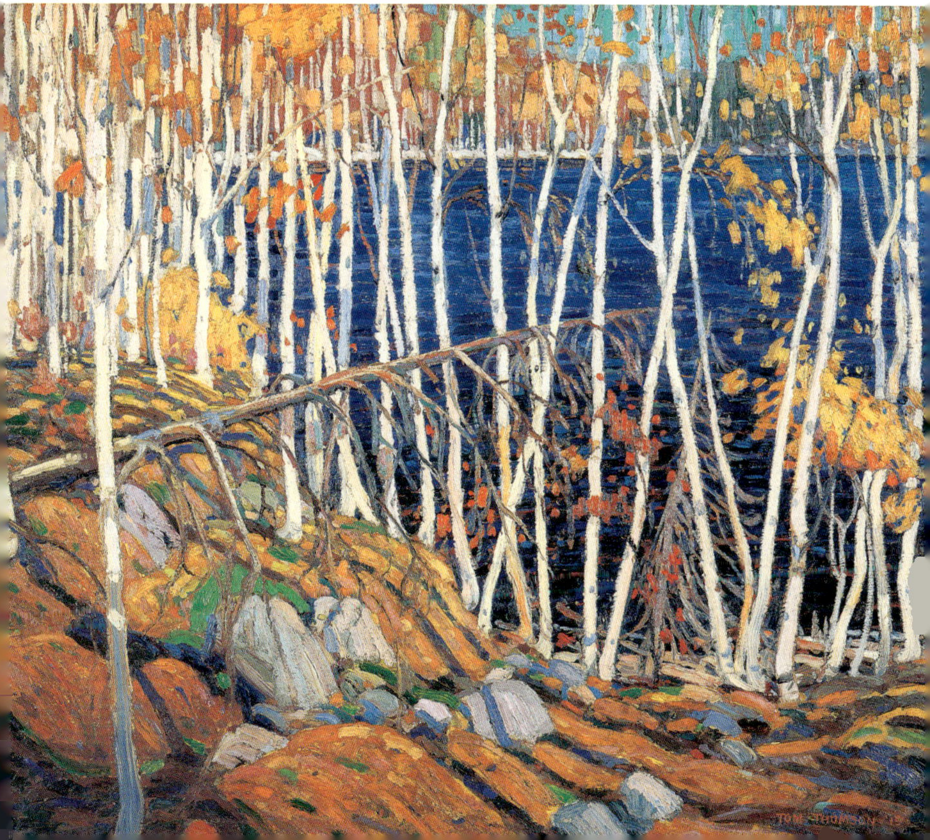

dark of the forest deeps. *Autumn's Garland* and *Opulent October* formed a decorative dyad, an idyll, a Canadian Arcadia. I imagine Tom was mystified when people found his pictures violent, frightening, inhuman. Inhuman?

"As if we are not every bit as much a part of the natural world as the lakes, hills, flowers, trees," he thought. He said nothing but remembered William Brodie's mantra: "Man, not apart, but a part of nature."

Harris goaded Tom into painting even more canvases, sneaking into his shack and placing blank canvases on Tom's easel. For *In the Northland* Tom used a square canvas as did Harris. He drew a fallen tree through the birch grove, to the wine-dark, rippled lake. Behind the grate of trees, beyond the cold lake; a sun-drenched beach, brilliant leaves, and green, an invitation to enter.

One Friday in December, M.O. Hammond, journalist and photographer, dropped by the Studio Building to visit the artists and claim a sketch from Beatty, long-owed, in return for photographs he had taken.

> Walked then over to Studio Building, Severn St., called on Williamson. He was genial and talkative. His place was untidy, cluttered a good deal. He had pictures of MacIntosh and T. Eaton under way. Both are good as far as done.
>
> Then he took me out to a shack at the back where Tom Thomson has his studio. T, whom I now first met, is a ~~tall~~ medium-sized, well-built chap, with a clean face, and the hard hands of the woodsman. But the place was awfully bare. He (and) Lismer work together and both are almost bankrupt. There was no fire in the stove. He explained it did not draw well for lack of enough pipe. But I perceive the real reason is no money for fuel. He showed me bunches of sketches by Jackson (and) Lismer, praised them highly but said nothing of himself save in answer to questions.[244]
>
> –M.O. Hammond Journal, Friday, December 10, 1915

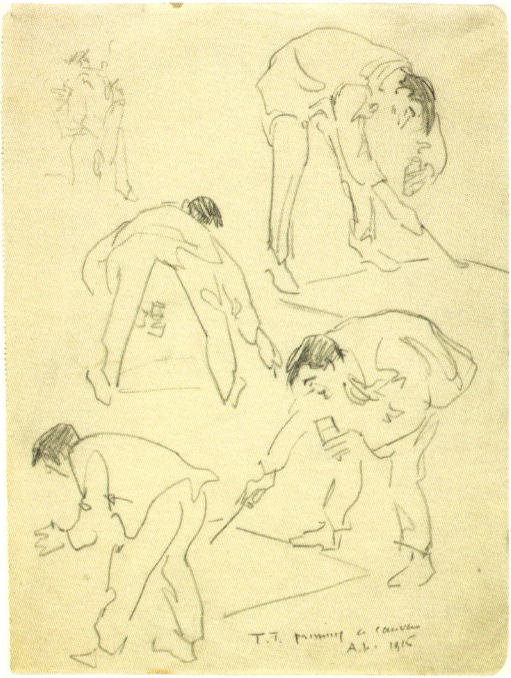

Arthur Lismer, *TT priming a canvas,* National Gallery of Canada

Afterwards, Hammond called on Heming then Beatty, the latter in a typically foul mood. He started in at once, fulminating against Heming who he said was being "grubstaked" by D.A. Dunlop, part owner of La Rose mine. It grieved him that Heming was comfortable while Thomson, so much a better painter, "Hasn't $50 between him and starvation...I'd give $50 if I could smash his head."[245]

At the turn of the year—at thirty-eight years of age—Tom had his first one-man show at the Arts and Letters Club, another shortly thereafter at the Heliconian Club, a club for female artists made necessary by their exclusion from organizations like the Arts and Letters Club. Women would not be considered "persons" under Canadian law for another thirteen years.

Artist and critic Estelle Kerr wrote a glowing review for Tom in *The Courier*:

> *Landscapes of Northern Ontario* by Tom Thomson form a striking exhibition which may be seen at the Heliconian Club. Mr. Thomson is considered one of the most promising painters who follows (the) Impressionist Movement, and his work reveals him to be a fine colourist, a clever technician, and a truthful interpreter of the north land in its various aspects.[246]

By the start of 1916, three hundred thousand Canadians had enlisted. Prime Minister Robert Borden had promised two hundred thousand more. Britain had enacted conscription; Canada, as yet, had not. In the papers and on the streets, shirkers and slackers were called out, abused:

> Don't you hear the bugle
> calling; calling for good men and true
> To take up their stand for
> freedom? That call is meant for you.
> Some boyhood chum has
> fallen and as he stricken lies
> He appeals to you to take
> his place in the glorious enterprise.
> Don't you mind my lads
> how promptly you joined in their
> games of yore?
> Don't let them call you
> slacker in the sterner game of war.
> And if in nobly striving the
> brave sacrifice you pay,
> Your chums will proudly tell
> the world that you died the British way.[247]

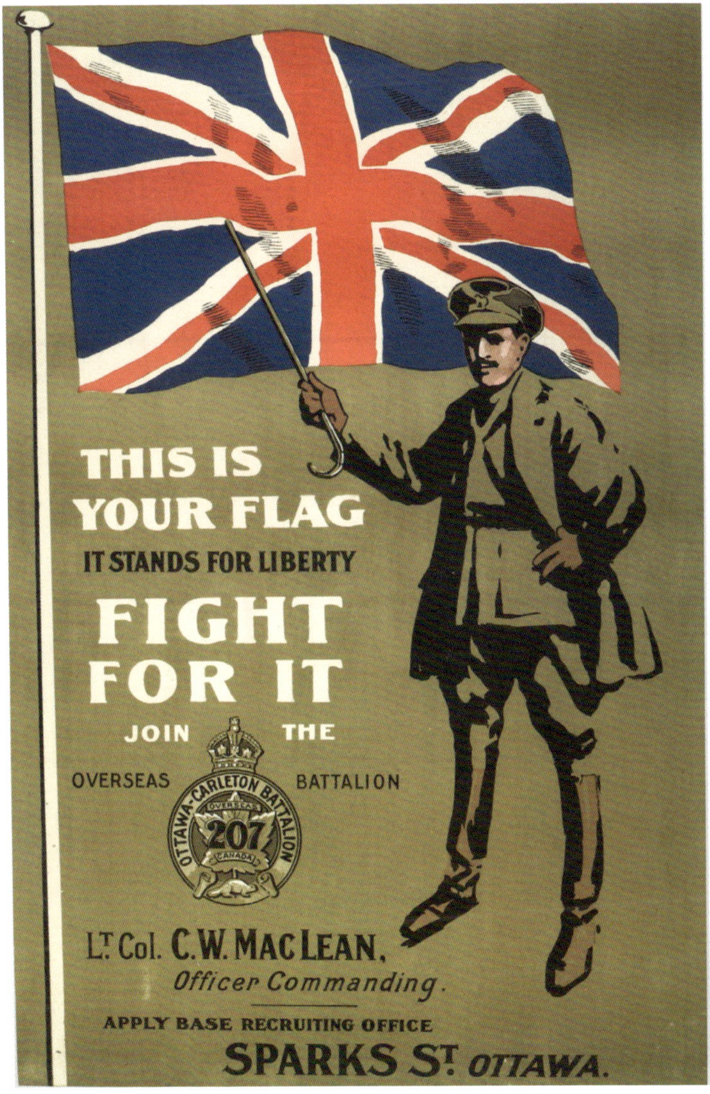

World War I Recruitment Poster, Canada, Canadian War Museum

Tom left for the park in March, just as the furor erupted over that year's Ontario Society of Artists show:

> The forty-fourth yearly exhibition of the Ontario Society of Artists opens today in the Art Museum gallery, on the corner of College and St. George streets. On the whole, the work of the younger men dominates the galleries, not so much as to numbers, but as to forcefulness, as to their use of strong, even violent, colour—colour that makes the quieter toned canvases look weak by comparison.[248]
>
> –M.L.A.F. (Margaret Fairbairn) "Some Pictures at the Art Gallery" *Toronto Daily Star, Mar. 11, 1916*

> Applied or quasi-futurism has gotten hold of the hanging committee of the Ontario Society of Artists this year with a strange clinch, and those who believe that pictures should be seen and not heard are likely to have their sensibilities shocked....It is, perhaps, one of the duties of the artist to surprise us and take us out of mental ruts, but it is hardly necessary to tear one's eyes out in the performance of that duty.
>
> The chief grudge that one has against these experimental pictures is that they almost destroy the effect of very meritorious and sincere pictures, which are hung on the same walls.[249]
>
> –Hector Charlesworth "Pictures That Can Be Heard" *Saturday Night Magazine*, Mar. 18, 1916

> Of these, Mr. (J.E.H) MacDonald's *A Tangled Garden* is a good example. It is what one might call "an incoherent mass of colour," for at first glance it seems a purposeless medley of crude colours which gradually explain themselves as standing for the blooms in a garden bed in full sunlight.[250]
>
> –Fairbairn

> The chief offender seems to be J.E.H. MacDonald.... his *Tangled Garden,* which a discriminating spectator attempted to praise by saying it was not half as bad as it looked.[251]
>
> –Charlesworth

> Mr. Tom Thomson('s) *The Birches* and *Hard Woods* show a fondness for intense yellows and orange and strong blue, altogether a fearless use of violent colour which can scarcely be called pleasing, yet which scoops an exaggeration of truthful feeling that time will temper.[252]
>
> –Fairbairn

> MacDonald has also infected a number of other talented young artists, who seem to think that crudity of colour and brushwork signify the vaunted qualities of "strength" and "self-expression.[253]
>
> –Charlesworth

Charlesworth excoriated several of MacDonald's pictures, retitled them "Hungarian Goulash," "Drunkard's Stomach." He reiterated old accusations, recycled paint pots, as if the Armory Show had never happened. Those who forget the past are condemned to repaint it.

Once again, MacDonald dashed off an angry rejoinder:

> We have a new country and a country practically unexplored artistically and it would seem therefore that courageous and thorough experiment is not only legitimate but vital to the development of a living Canadian art.[254]
>
> –*The Globe,* March 15, 1916

Although many artists were supportive of the fledgling school, many established artists, already jealous of the attention MacDonald and his friends had garnered, were galled by the implication that their artistic explorations of Canada did not count.

Painter and critic Carl Ahrens launched a far more personal attack:

> *The so-called new art has no excuse, it bespeaks of a hermaphroditic condition of the mind. These young people who are indulging in these pastimes would gain a much higher standing before men if they gave up their now misspent efforts to the destruction of the Hun.*[255]

Hermaphroditic here means homosexual. At this time in Canada, sodomy was punishable by life in prison.

Tom was embittered by the artists' in-fighting, the apathetic public, the vicious critics, although not only had he avoided the worst of the criticism, but also the National Gallery actually bought *Spring Ice* for $300, no mean feat in the throes of wartime cutbacks.

In April, Tom was up in Algonquin again, joined by Lawren Harris, Harris's cousin Chester and Dr. MacCallum. The men canoed and camped together. Tom took them to the north end of Algonquin Park: Little Cauchon Lake and Aura Lee Lake. Harris recounted:

> *I remember one afternoon in early spring on the shore of one of the Cauchon Lakes in Algonquin Park when a dramatic thunderstorm came up. There was a wild rush of wind across the lake and all nature was tossed into a turmoil. Tom and I were in an abandoned lumber shack. When the storm broke, Tom looked out, grabbed his sketch box, ran out into the gale, squatted behind a big stump and commenced to paint in a fury.*[256]

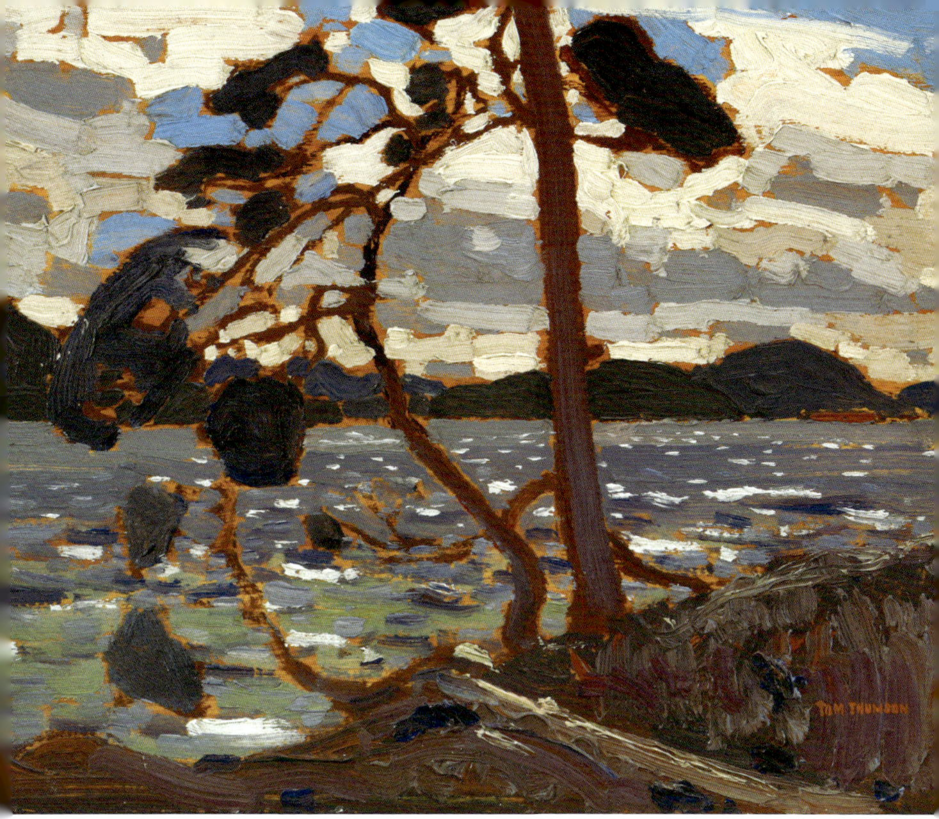

Tom Thomson, Sketch of "The West Wind," 1916, Art Gallery of Ontario

Picture this: *Tom's hair is plastered to his head; his green mackinaw jacket soaks up water like a sponge. A sudden burst of wind topples the stump on Tom, a massive wooden hand smacking a mosquito. Harris calls out in alarm, "Tom! Tom!" For a moment there is no sign of life then Tom hops up, waves and continues to paint—a twisted pine, bent like a lyre, a robin's egg blue sky contending with piebald clouds, a whitecapped lake, distant hillocks loitering grey and green. But the damned clouds moved too fast to capture, and the trunk cuts between shorelines, barring the way in.*

Make me thy lyre, ev'n as the forest is:
What if my leaves are falling like its own!
The tumult of thy mighty harmonies
Will take from both a deep autumnal tone,
Sweet though in sadness. Be thou, Spirit fierce,
My spirit! be thou me, impetuous one!
Drive my dead thoughts over the universe,
Like wither'd leaves, to quicken a new birth;
And, by the incantation of this verse,
Scatter, as from an unextinguish'd hearth
Ashes and sparks, my words among mankind!
Be through my lips to unawaken'd earth
The trumpet of a prophecy! O Wind,
If Winter comes, can Spring be far behind?"[257]

–Percy Bysshe Shelley, *"The West Wind"*

Later, when Tom spotted a weathered pine on the shore of Little Cauchon Lake, it transported him to a summer years before as he walked in Toronto's High Park with his elderly cousin, William Brodie, dead these six years.

"Fires are a natural part of forest life, necessary even, for its continuance," says Brodie raising his bushy eyebrows emphatically. "Take the Jack pine, for instance, *Pinus banksiana*, it requires intense heat for the cones to open, only then do the seeds scatter, germinate. Like the phoenix eh? Born in flames. You don't want to eradicate fires, merely to contain them, survive them."

Tom sat, quickly sketched the upright trunk, the scraggly limbs, bits of pines to left and right, a lake like glass reflecting the prismatic sky above.

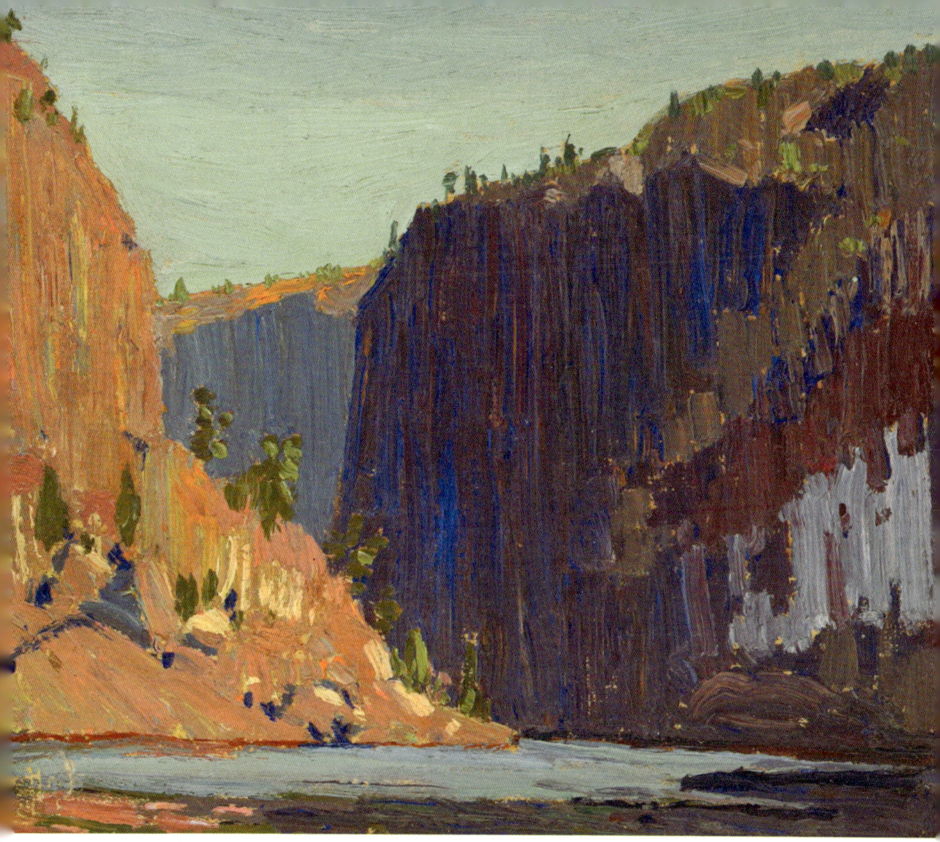

Tom Thomson, *Petawawa Gorges,* McMichael Canadian Art Collection

In May, Tom headed out to Achray Station on Grand Lake, at the south branch of the Petawawa River in the park's east end, fire ranging with Ed Godin. The two men canoed the rapid rivers, cataracts pinioned between massive walls of rock. On steep hills they set up lookouts, laddered steps against the tallest white pines and kept the portages clear so people could get around in case of fire. They met with railway men whose locomotives had started many of the fires.

In August, Tom and Godin canoed down the south branch of the Petawawa where Tom sketched *Petawawa Gorges* as he had in 1914, but this time without the guidance and companionship of A.Y. Jackson—massive clay-coloured bluffs, royal blue in the shade. A pine-covered outcropping slopes into the grey-blue water, beckoning, "canoe around the bend."

They followed the Booth Company timber drive, lakes jammed with bobbing logs, frothy water spewing from the chute. They spoke to the men about fire safety and watched how they handled the log booms. Tom sketched *Bateaux, Sandbank with Logs, The Alligator, Algonquin Park*, and *Log Jam.*

Back in Huntsville, Canoe Lake cottager and Tom's would-be girlfriend, Winnie Trainor, and her mother knitted socks for soldiers and raised money for the troops with Women's Temperance Union at All Saints' Anglican. She wondered why Tom couldn't fire range closer to her family's cottage, especially after a Grand Trunk engine ignited a pile of wood chips at nearby Canoe Lake train station.

Early June in Montreal, A.Y. Jackson's mother received a terse telegram:

> **Government cable, June 4th, 1916**
> Sincerely regret to inform you 457396 Private Alexander Jackson infantry officially reported admitted No. 1 Canadian General Hospital Etaples gunshot wound hip.[258]

Jackson was shipped first to the French coast and then back to England. He soon recovered and was digging latrines and peeling potatoes until he was drafted into a division of Canadian war artists, later joined by Varley. Tom might have been chosen to become a war artist, too, but it was only in the summer of 1917 that Canadian artists were commissioned by Lord Beaverbrook to paint the Canadian war effort, and by then, Tom was dead.

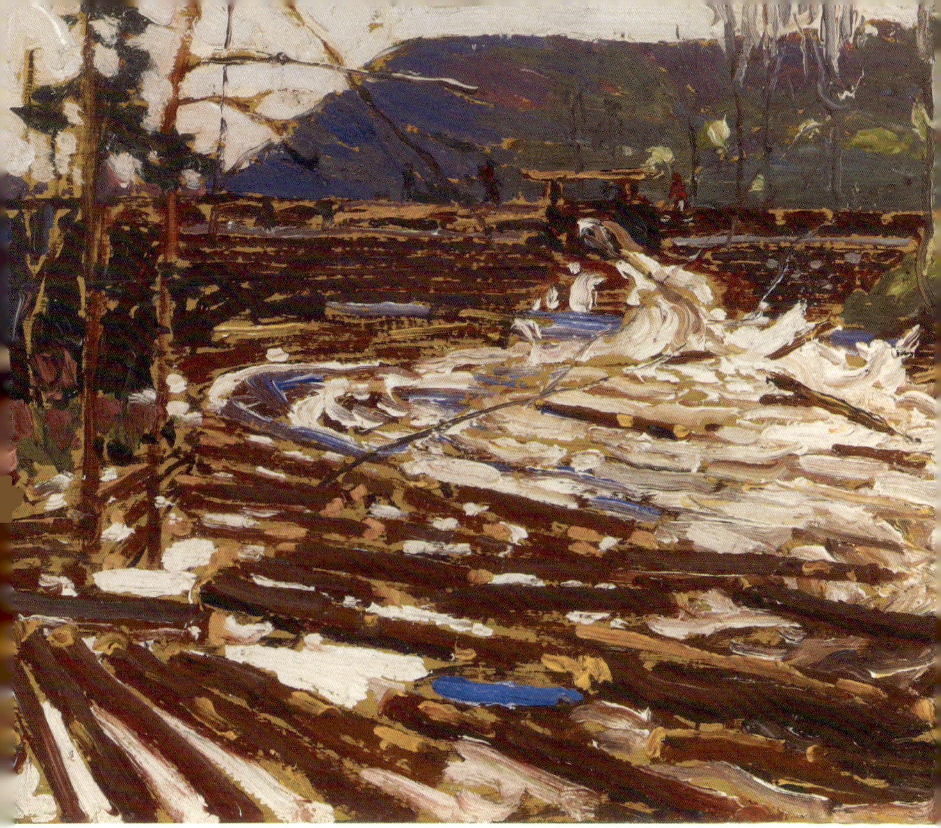

Tom Thomson, *Log Jam: Sketch for "The Drive,"* 1916, The Thomson Collection at the Art Gallery of Ontario

Back in Toronto, the Canadian National Exhibition once again featured a model military camp. The 169th Battalion from Camp Borden set up camp just west of the Transportation Building. In addition to demonstrations of trench warfare there were special details of grenade throwers, bombers and bayonet squads. On nearby Lake Ontario, miniature battleships dodged submarine mines and airplane bombs while firing torpedoes at each other. Tom's *Moonlight* is featured in the catalogue, as well as in the gallery, at that year's Ex.

Tom wrote Dr. MacCallum:

Have done very little sketching this summer as I find that the two jobs don't fit in. When we are traveling two go together—one for the canoe and the other, the pack, and there's no place for a sketch outfit when you're fire ranging. It would be great for two artists or whatever you call us but the natives can't see what we paint for. We are not fired yet but I am hoping to be put off right away.[259]

In October, the fire ranging ended. Tom stayed near Achray, began to paint in earnest. Time stood still when Tom painted; he lost any sense of himself, immersed entirely in the painting. He doesn't think about what he is doing; if he did, he'd second guess, analyze and the sketch would be lost. Instead, he found the scene then went on instinct; told himself "don't think, paint." It's addictive, this loss of self. No self means no doubts, no frustration, no worries about money, no loneliness. Tom made sketch after sketch, paints on both sides of the board; when he runs out of boards, he uses orange crates.[260]

Back at Canoe Lake, Tom made some extra cash hauling stones from Sim's Pit to Little Wap Island to make a fireplace for cottager Taylor Statten—an eerie foreshadowing of Bill Beatty's labours the following autumn, hauling stones like an ill-tempered Sisyphus to the top of Hayhurst Point for Tom's cairn.

Tom visited Winnie Trainor at her cabin and again in Huntsville before he left for Toronto. "You know I can't stay Winnie. My studio is in Toronto, my colleagues, all the shows are there, and the buyers too."

At the Royal Canadian Academy of Arts show in November, J.E.H. MacDonald's garden sketch continued to infuriate critics. The Hot Mushers were accused of making "freak art."

Tom returned to Toronto to find his few remaining friends had scattered. Lawren Harris had enlisted in the spring and was now a musketry instructor at Camp Borden near Barrie, Ontario. Conditions there were so dismal that the troops called it "Camp Horror" and rioted at its official opening. Tom's daytime shackmate, Arthur Lismer, was now the principal of the Victoria School of Art and Design in Halifax, Nova Scotia, a posting Bill Beatty had refused but would later come to covet, writing letters suggesting Lismer should be let go in favour of him.

Tom's former studiomate, Franklin Carmichael, had gone back to full-time commercial work at Rous and Mann Press and moved his family to the suburb of Thornhill, like Tom's mentor, J.E.H. MacDonald, who was surviving on freelance work such as decorating the windows of Simpson's department store in Toronto for Christmas.

Tom's canvases that year were larger and more numerous than ever. Even without Harris' good-natured goading, Tom painted up canvas after canvas in Harris' square dimensions, winter matching the productivity of fall.

Tom struggled with the sky in *West Wind.* He couldn't capture it in the sketch and failed with the canvas as well, scraped and repainted but couldn't get it right. Tom abandoned that canvas and began work on *The Jack Pine,* starting with an undercoat of burnt sienna, a sanguine aura for the trees, the distant shore. Tom roughed in the central tree. How human it is, like Christ at Calvary, leafy thieves on either side. But it's more a *pieta* than a crucifixion scene by the attitude of

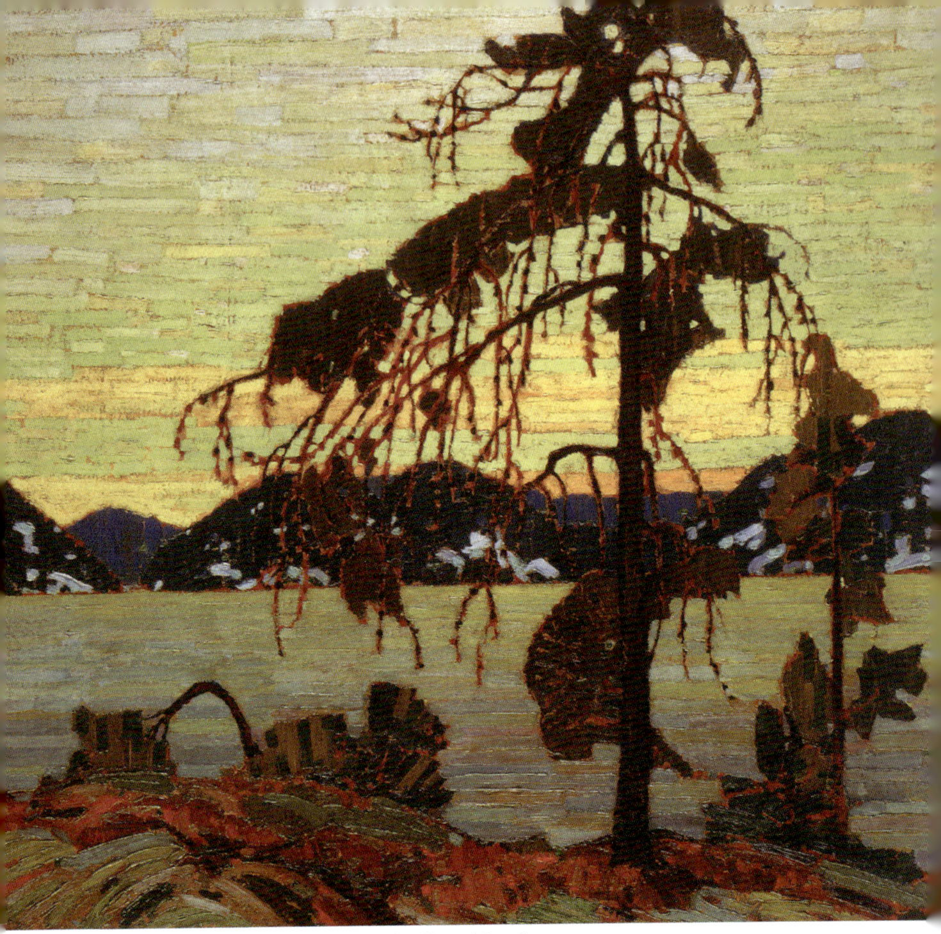

Tom Thomson, *The Jack Pine,* National Gallery of Canada

the tree's limbs. The longest bough, lolls to the left, or is it gesturing towards the distant shore? A signpost? Tom adds an ingress to the shore, a space between the royal blue hills, a passage through to the distant cobalt shore, an invitation to enter. In fact, it's more than an invitation; it's a truth told, "Man is a part of nature, not apart from it." Tom transposed the sky and the reflective lake face, from his sketch *A Lake in Autumn* to *The Jack Pine*—horizontal lines in a spectrum of greens and yellows.

Picture this: As Tom stares at his masterpiece, the chemical wedding of his lithe art deco and staccato sketching styles, he floats past the outstretched limb, over the still, sky-streaked lake, through the narrows to that far distant cobalt shore.

Although Tom was dissatisfied with his canvas for *West Wind*, the image of a lone pine twisting in the wind in front of a whitecapped lake burned into Tom's former co-worker Franklin Carmichael's inner eye, Fred Varley's as well, and Lismer's too, once he sees it.[261] It becomes a template for their future works, just as J.W. Beatty's *The Evening Cloud of the Northland* had for Tom many years before. This image became eidetic, a blueprint for generations of Canadian artists, burning into the inner eye of a nation. It became a touchstone for a people, an icon undying.

Tom spent the Christmas of 1916 with his family in Owen Sound. He attended a dance at Leith Hall with his sister Lizzie and her family. His parents and sister Peggy were home, sick with the flu.

Back in Toronto, J.E.H. MacDonald's teenage son, Thoreau, visited Tom at his shack:

> *Sometimes he invited me to stay for meals and I remember well the woodsman's flourish with which he threw a handful of tea into the pot and mashed the potatoes with an empty bottle, adding what looked like half a pound of butter. While we ate he drummed his fingers on the table with great speed and vigor. I suppose he was anxious for me to go so that he could get to his work again.*

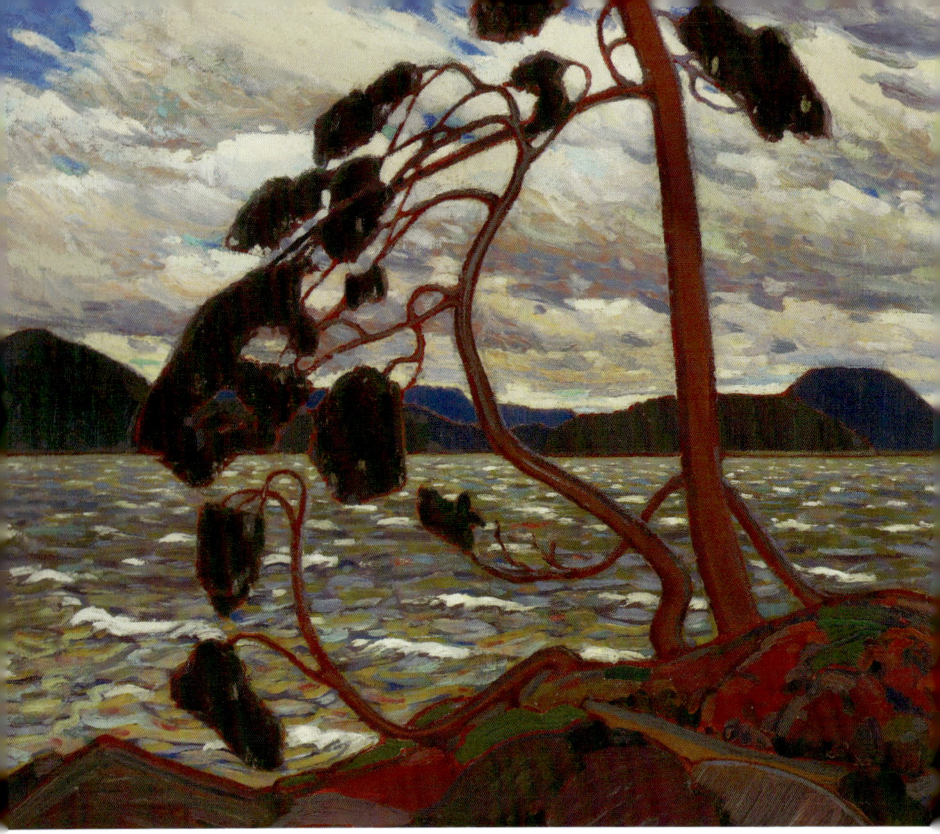

Tom Thomson, *The West Wind*, 1916–1917, Art Gallery of Ontario

> *He must have felt me a nuisance in many ways, for often I tried to persuade him to come to Thornhill and go snowshoeing or shoot at a mark with our .22. He always had some excuse, even claiming if he went away his fire would go out and his preserves would freeze.*[262]

Although he drummed his fingers impatiently, Tom listened politely to the boy's prattle, thinking, "How much like his father he looks." Idly Tom wondered what his son would look like, if he had one. If he and Alice Lambert had married, he could have had a twelve-year old by now. If he'd married Elizabeth McCarnen, he could have had a ten-year old.

Florence McGillivray also visited Tom's shack that winter. Newly returned from Europe, Tom knew her through her art. She'd shown her paintings at the OSA and RCA shows—modern, bold, colourful in the French post-impressionist tradition.

McGillivray had taken art lessons from Cruikshank, like Tom, and was born in Whitby, near Tom's birthplace of Claremont. McGillivray had taught art at a girl's school in Whitby, but at 49 years of age had left to study art in Paris with Lucien Simon and Émile René Ménard. When she returned to Canada, she sought out members of the arts community and was directed to Tom, a promising new artist also working in a post-impressionist style.

Inspecting Tom's sketches around the shack, his canvases, she commented on the vitality, the strength, but unlike many others, she didn't find them foreign or foreboding. Instead, she found them invigorating, compelling, a destination worth visiting. Tom would later tell his friend, ranger Mark Robinson, "She is the first of the artists I know to recognize instantly what I am trying to do."[263]

Doctor MacCallum was another visitor that winter. He found Tom hard at work on a large canvas filled with brilliant daubs of paint, red boats on a lake, part of the timber drive:

> *Tom Thomson used color and brush stroke in a dozen different ways—he had no system—was unconscious of any system—thought only of what he was feeling and trying to express. I have more of his work than any person or institution, from his earliest days to his last—method he had none, or rather he had dozen—but he never thought about the method.*
>
> *Watching him sketching one day I said, "Tom how do you know that these Jabs and dots you are putting down is going to look like a real thing*[?]" *His reply was, "Why it*

> *looks just like that!" You have not seen the* Pointers *(or the* Pageant of the North*)—done in big blotches of pure colour 2 inches by ¾* [of an inch]*—some larger, some smaller. This was done in this way because the critics had been attacking him and his methods. When I dropped in on him while he was painting it and asked him why he was doing it in that way his answer was, "Damn them! I'll show them."*[264]

In March 1917, Tom attended Florence McGillivray's one-woman show at painter Harry Britton's house, 67 Wellesley Street in Toronto. He was there not as a follower of MacDonald's nor as a protégé of Jackson's, but as a peer, a fellow painter, a friend of the artist. Rather than chucking the invite afterwards, Tom kept it in his sketch box, a memento, a reminder.

It was not a lack of confidence that kept Tom from submitting a canvas to the OSA in 1917. He was done with the critics, the bickering artists, done with the cash-strapped public galleries, the apathetic public. Although he had sold paintings at every OSA since 1912, he decided it was not worth the stress. "The government has cut its budgets and a sale is no sure thing. It's the painting, not the sales that matter, and that is where I'll focus my energies," he decided.

While the U.S.A. joined the war effort at last and flying Ace Billy Bishop marked his first kill, Tom returned to Algonquin Park. There he was reunited with ranger Mark Robinson who had returned from the war, invalided by a minor injury. Tom got his guide's license, though there were precious few tourists again that year, and dug a garden for the Frasers and the Trainors, in whose cabin his sketches would be stored.

The Crombies were staying at Mowat Lodge when Tom arrived. Robin, a young soldier "taking the cure" in Algonquin Park for the tuberculosis that sent him home from the war, and Daphne, his newlywed wife, celebrating their honeymoon by nursing her ailing spouse.

> *I'd go out and sit with Robin and talk, all wrapped up in the cold. When he'd get drowsy, I'd go in the old dining room at Mowat Lodge, and there was Tom Thomson painting. I'd just sit quietly and wouldn't say a word until Tom talked to me, because I knew he didn't want to be disturbed.*
>
> *The only ones that were there were Robin and I, we had our rooms on the far side of Mowat. Then there was the middle room, and then over on this side was Tom's room upstairs. He always joined us at night. He was a rather moody, quiet chap, and rather withdrawn. When I was with him, he'd talk away because we were pals.*[265]

Daphne watched Tom make sketch after sketch. Sometimes he acknowledged her presence:

> *I was very interested in his painting. He would tell me about it. He would say, "Now you see that bit of light down there, now where does that come from? Is that the true light? Now you have to get the true shade of light there that is coming down from the sky."*
>
> *I asked Tom why his shadows were so blue. He said, "tomorrow morning you go out at about 11 and go up the pathway, and just notice them." When I would go out and the sun was coming down straight, the shadows weren't really as blue as Tom made them, but when I came back a little while later, there was quite a difference in the shade of the shadows.*[266]

When Daphne Crombie returned from a walk with a bouquet of pussy willows, Tom offered to make her a vase. He painted a mason jar with his precious oil paints.

> *He was so nice about making me this jam jar. He painted these things all the way around the jar for me when Annie broke the one I'd had. He also said that he wanted me to take the painting I liked best. I told him to choose it, because he was the expert.*
>
> *He evidently admired me because he gave me the painting of the year. I was a bride looking after my husband as I say.*[267]

Tom's brother-in-law, Tom Harkness, sent him an article from the local paper by mail:

> In every report concerning pictures exhibited by Ontario's artists in Toronto for the past few years there has been a paragraph or sentence which, without exception, was one of praise for the pictures shown by Mr. Tom Thomson. He has been spoken of by the highest art critics as a young artist who is on the threshold of an exceptionally brilliant career, and any work he shows always receives marked praise.
>
> A member of The Sun staff had the pleasure, while in Toronto recently of paying a visit to Mr. Thomson's winter studio in Rosedale, and the visit was all that was needed to convince one that Mr. Thomson is indeed an artist whose name will be much before the public in coming years.[268]
>
> –"Pictures by Sydenham Boy Worth Seeing,"
> *The Owen Sound–Sun*, Apr. 10, 1917

After Tom read the article, he fired off a reply to his brother-in-law: "I got a copy of the *O.S. Sun* and it seemed to be well filled with bunk, however, the foolishness of newspaper matter is well known and I knew nothing about it in time to have it stopped."[269]

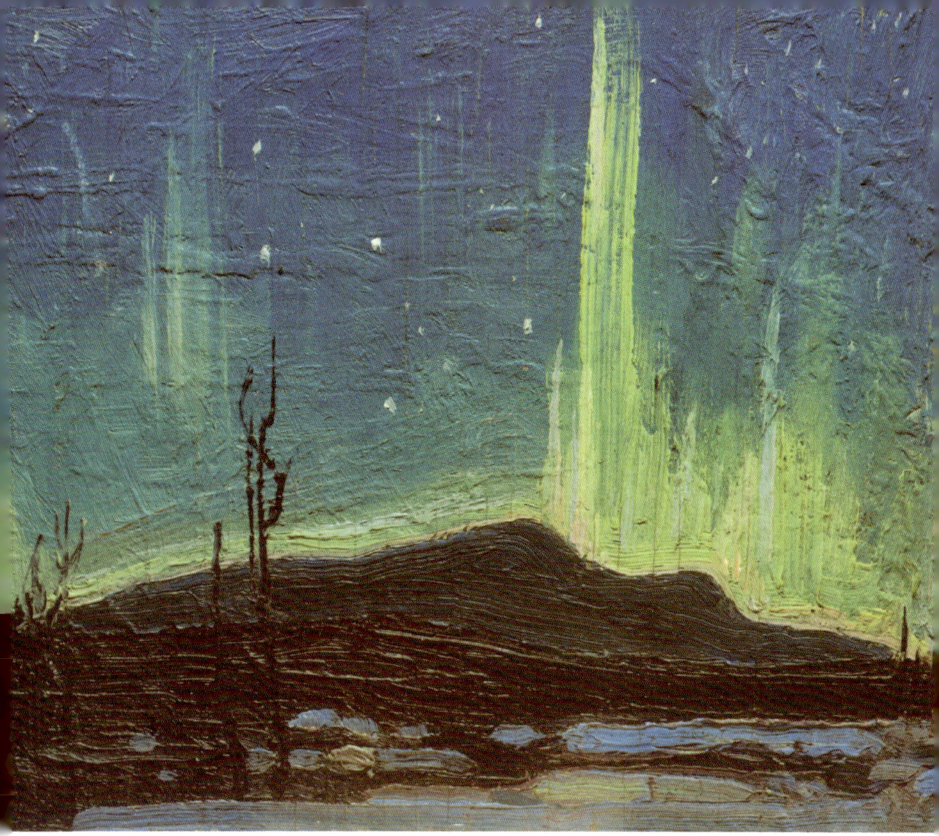

Tom Thomson, *Northern Lights,* National Gallery of Canada

One night, after sunset, Tom saw the fairy green shimmer of the Northern Lights. He could almost hear its sizzling song. He called on Robinson at his cabin, a short distance from Mowat Lodge. "Did you see the lights?" "Yes, Tom," said Robinson, "they're brilliant tonight." Tom warmed his hands over the fire, left to watch the lights, returned to thaw out again. Finally, about eleven-thirty Tom announced, "I believe I can paint that up." "Alright," said Robinson, "I'll keep the fire on for you." Tom smiled wistfully, "Oh, there's no background here."[270]

Tom trudged down to the point where Larry Dickson and George Rowe's cottage stood. He set a fire, stepped outside to paint at midnight. Massive green flames undulated across the night sky. The stillness, the eerie quiet of the earth was in stark contrast to the living sky.

Before the Crombies left, Daphne and Annie Fraser—Mowat Lodge's cook and also proprietor Shannon Fraser's wife—walked by Larry Dickson's cabin.

Tom shouted, "Stop. Stay where you are."[271] The women wait while Tom painted them into the sketch.

Doctor MacCallum and his young son Arthur took the train up to Canoe Lake Station for a rainy and cold fishing trip one weekend in May. The doctor "threw Tom a bone," admitting that Algonquin Park is a better place to paint than his cottage: "...in the Georgian Bay there is in the spring practically none of the brilliant colour from the vegetation of the park—there were really only two soft maples in bud—the birches have not even begun to change."[272]

It was a cold and wet spring. When the ice went out, the black flies and mosquitoes came in worse than ever, even "bug dope" didn't dissuade them. Despite this, Tom remained as prolific as he had been the previous winter and fall, painting at least one sketch a day.

He told Robinson, "I have a record of the weather for sixty-two days, rain or shine, snow, dark or bright. I have a record of the day in a sketch.[273]"

In terms of sheer output, Tom's work rivaled A.Y. Jackson's hero, Vincent van Gogh, who had produced seventy paintings, in the last seventy days of his life.

The cold and wet spring gave way to a cool and damp summer. The fishing, however, was good, and Tom and Robinson shared a good-natured rivalry over a monstrous trout.

"For about ten days before his death there were several of us trying to invent a lure that would entice a wily old trout that frequented a pool below Joe Lake Dam. Tom was there every day and several times had hooked the trout but never landed him. I had about the same luck and it was a good-natured contest as to which of us would land the trout."[274]

On July 7, Tom wrote Dr. MacCallum.

I am still around Frasers and have not done any sketching since the flies started. The weather has been wet and cold all spring and the flies and mosquitos much worse than I have seen them any year and fly dope doesn't have any effect on them. This however is the second warm day we have had this year and another day or so like this will finish them.

Will send my winter sketches down in a day or two and have every intention of making some more but it has been impossible lately.

Have done a great deal of paddling this spring and the fishing has been fine. Have done some guiding for fishing parties and will have some other trips this month and next with probably some sketching in between.[275]

It was raining on the morning of July 8, 1917; Robinson recalled that Shannon Fraser and Thomson went after the "wily old trout" near Joe Lake Dam.

On the morning of his death he almost got the old trout and as he missed it he said, "I am going to one of the little lakes and get a trout and put it on Mark's doorstep early in the morning and he will think it's the old fish from the dam."[276]

> *They returned to Mowat Lodge. Thomson got out his canoe. He had no bread. Fraser went up to the Lodge got him a loaf and Thomson stowed it away, with a can of corn syrup, under the bow of the canoe.*[277]

Tom set off in his canoe that afternoon and was never seen alive again.

Ninety-five years earlier, to the day, July 8, 1822, Percy Bysshe Shelley the poet, author of "The West Wind," drowned in the blood-warm Mediterranean Sea at the tender age of thirty.

Picture this: Although it was midday, Canoe Lake has a morning calm, mirror-smooth lake reflecting sky reflecting lake ad infinitum. Past Little Wap Island, an unexpected mist lifts off the lake. Though they are difficult to make out, Tom sees what looks like two deer, a buck and doe, white as snow, on the shore, likely trees, bowed survivors of countless conflagrations, winter storms. Tom canoes towards them. Through the haze, he sees a narrows between two pine-covered hills, a passage through to a distant blue shore, an ingress, an invitation.

> Some said to hill, and some to glen,
> Their wonderous course had been;
> But ne'er in the haunts of living men
> Again was Thomas seen. [278]

At 3:00 PM Tom's canoe was found overturned, three-quarters of a mile from where he set out. Eight days later, his body was found. He was buried in the little cemetery at Canoe Lake. Cottager Martin Blecher Sr. read the service.

At the request of his family, he was disinterred and reburied at Leith, or was supposed to be, sharing a grave with his infant brother, James, and his maternal grandfather, Kenneth Matheson.

When he heard the news, A.Y. Jackson wrote J.E.H. MacDonald:

> *I have heard nothing further about Tom, but conclude it is only too true. I know how keenly you will feel his loss. You had very much in common. Tom, though he was a man of few words, often expressed his confidence in you and in the future of your work, and without you he never would have associated himself with our little school. Well, it is a blessing that the last years of his life were devoted as they were. He has blazed a trail where others may follow, and we will never go back to the old days again.*[279]

Back in Toronto, in Thornhill, in England, in Halifax, Tom's friends mourned. They promoted his work, showed it along with their own, ensuring any profits went to his parents and siblings. Tom's family mourned as well. Peggy Thomson wrote Dr. MacCallum:

> *Our hearts are still almost broken and I don't know whether our sorrow will ever wear away or not. His death was the first break in our large grown up family. Tom seemed to have a place in each of our hearts, that could not be filled by any one else. He was so good and so kind and he seemed almost perfect in every way.*
>
> *He was so much alone that we seemed to think more about him than any of the others of the family. Poor boy, he worked so hard, denied himself so much and now to think he is gone.*

It is one of my regrets now, that I hadn't written to him more often. I had intended writing to him quite often this summer, and I was going to send him margarine and boxes of homemade cooking, but it seems I have been denied this pleasure. I am sure many a time he must have been lonely when out in the wilds.[280]

Although Lawren Harris and J.E.H. MacDonald were broken for a time—a nervous breakdown and a stroke—and A.Y. Jackson and Fred Varley were overseas, the Hot Mushers would persevere. They would become the legendary Group of Seven, the preeminent school of painters in Canada for the 20th century.

A decade after Tom's death, their foothold in Canada established, The Group of Seven exhibited in England, the motherland, to great acclaim.

> Canada has not only gained artistic independence, but can boast of a real national school that owes little or nothing to European influence, is racy of the soil, and expresses Canadian Landscape and Canadian life in an idiom of its own. Canadian art has progressed with rapid strides.
>
> Not more than seven years ago, when I visited Toronto and Montreal, the pioneers of this movement, the "Group of Seven" who had just lost their leader, Tom Thomson, the artistic "discoverer" of Canadian landscape, were still an isolated clique fighting bravely against the prejudice of the ignorant public. Now at Wembley, they have it all their own way. They practically fill the two rooms with their daring, decorative, and intensely stimulating landscapes.
>
> The movement seems to have attracted many new recruits in Toronto, and to have spread to Montreal. I know of no European school that shows such unity of effort, on a similar combination of nature-worship and respect for the laws that rule pictorial design, or a similar balance of representational element and abstract aesthetic principles, as are found in the work of these Canadians.[281]
>
> –*The Observer,* London, "The palace of arts at Wembley" by P.G. Konody, May 24, 1925

Despite many books about Thomson and his art, he remains as enigmatic and inaccessible as many found him in life: a solitary genius, remote, reticent,[282] an unschooled prodigy, "harsh, brittle, brilliant, uncouth."[283] Questions around his death, buzz about his life and art, distract from his accomplishments: hundreds of sketches, dozens of canvases in less than four years, a vibrant, startlingly original style that continues to influence artists, capture the imagination of a nation, a century after his death. Now Thomson's paintings adorn the walls of major Canadian galleries, tour the world to acclaim, adorn calendars, coffee mugs, t-shirts. The remaining private paintings are auctioned for millions, more than enough to "pay for some paint."

As with Yeats, elegized by Auden, Thomson "became his admirers."[284] He has been simplified in death, details erased, attributes and incidents harmonized to suit his biographer's designs.

The paintings though remain unchanged: Waves slap at the rocky shoreline, the wind takes form in the trees, the scent of the sun on the fallen pine needles. I urge you to visit the McMichael Gallery in Kleinberg, the National Gallery in Ottawa, the Art Gallery of Ontario in Toronto or any gallery that displays his work. Whether or not you think about Thomson, Brodie or Frye, just look. As you look, see if something inside you answers back. Consider whether something within you recognizes itself, is responding to an invitation. If you are so fortunate to receive such an invitation, I strongly urge you to accept.

Notes

Prologue

1 Letter from E. Harkness (nee Thomson) to J. MacCallum, (9 February 1918), in "Tom Thomson's Missing Sketch Box," *Algonquin Elegy* by Neil J. Lehto, "n.d.", (11 December 2018). <http://www.algonquinelegy.com/Box.html>.

2 "Canadian and Colonial Painting," in *The Bush Garden* by Frye, Northrop, House of Anansi, 1971.

3 Ibid.

4 Ibid.

5 Ibid.

6 As per the official road maps of Ontario, <http://www.mto.gov.on.ca/english/traveller/map/northindexpdf.shtml>.

7 "In 1898 George W. Bartlett was appointed as the second superintendent of Algonquin Park, replacing the late Peter Thompson. Placed under the direction of the Premier of Ontario to make the park self-sufficient, Bartlett worked to make the park more attractive to tourists by encouraging short-term leases for cottages, lodges, and camps." Wikipedia contributors. "Algonquin Provincial Park." Wikipedia, The Free Encyclopedia. *Wikipedia, The Free Encyclopedia*, 16 Nov. 2018. Web. 12 Dec. 2018.

8 Suzanne Zeller, "Brodie, William", *Dictionary of Canadian Biography*, vol. 13, University of Toronto/Université Laval, "1994", (January 19, 2016).

9 Genesis, 1:28.

10 Suzanne Zeller, "Brodie, William".

11 This quote is attributed to numerous authors. The earliest instance I have found is in from Jane Robert's 1963 novel The Rebellers, Ace Books.

12 As noted in Murray, *Tom Thomson: Design for a Canadian Hero*, Dundurn, 1998.

Chapter 1

13 I am drawing on the imagination of Angie Littlefield, *The Thomsons of Durham*, Envoy, 2005.

14 Davies states Thomson was quarantined in Montreal; perhaps the shacks on Grosse Isle were full, but I have no evidence to support this.

15 William Wood, *Past Years in Pickering*, William Briggs, 1911.

16 However, in a 1931 letter to Blodwen Davies, Minnie Thomson wrote, "I couldn't help thinking while reading the booklet that owing to lack of information which only the family could give, undue emphasis had been placed in the illiteracy of grandfather Thomson." "After all, judging by the Canadian educational standards of his day, grandfather was not illiterate. He could read and write and transact his business shrewdly and successfully. He had the three R's and that was as much education as many of the schoolteachers then had." Blodwen Davies fonds, Vol. 11, Library and Archives Canada, MG30.

17 Littlefield believes Margaret had met John in Whitby, and it was John who hired her to "help out" at Claremont.

18 Larsen has John say this in *Tom Thomson: Artist of the North*, Dundurn, 2011.

19 Littlefield believes the stone cottage was built first, and the two-storey house, after John and Margaret were married.

20 Ann Kelly, "Officially' Retired Organist Wilson Buzza, 74, a Storehouse of History." *Sun Times (Owen Sound)*, 12 January 1977.

Chapter 2

21 As described in Murray, *Tom Thomson: Design for a Canadian Hero*, Dundurn, 1998.

22 As quoted in a letter from Alan Ross to Blodwen Davies, 11 June 1930, Blodwen Davies fonds, Vol. 11, Library and Archives Canada, MG30.

23 Margaret Tweedale tells this anecdote to discredit story that Tom disliked Fraser. 6 September 1973, Library and Archives Canada, Harold Town fonds, Vol. 30, File 10, MG30 D404.

24 As described in letter from Minnie Thomson to Blodwen Davies, 11 March 1931, Blodwen Davies fonds, Vol. 11, Library and Archives Canada, MG30.

25 As described in an interview by Joan Murray with Margaret Thomson Tweedale, 12 February 1971, typed hand notes, Joan Murray Tom Thomson Papers.

26 Ibid.

27 As described in Silcox and Town, *Tom Thomson, The Silence and the Storm*, Firefly Books, 2001.

28 As described in letter from Louise Thomson to Davies, 11 March 1931, Blodwen Davies fonds, Vol. 11, Library and Archives Canada, MG30.

29 Quoted from a letter from Minnie Thomson to Davies, 2 February 1931, Blodwen Davies fonds, Vol. 11, Library and Archives Canada, MG30.

30 As described in a letter from Louise Thomson to Davies, 11 March 1931, Blodwen Davies fonds, Vol. 11, Library and Archives Canada, MG30.

31 Ibid.

32 Quoted from a letter from Ross to Davies, 11 June 1930, Blodwen Davies fonds, Vol. 11, Library and Archives Canada, MG30.

33 Ibid. "I remember my sister Maggie, who was a school teacher (she died in 1909, poor girl) once telling me that she never knew any who could concentrate on a task given him at school like his brother Ralph could."

34 As described in a letter from Minnie Thomson to Davies, 2 February 1931, Blodwen Davies fonds, Vol. 11, Library and Archives Canada, MG30.

35 Quoted from a letter from Louise Thomson to Davies, 11 March 1931, Blodwen Davies fonds, Vol. 11, Library and Archives Canada, MG30.

36 Ibid.

37 Quoted from a letter described in a letter from Minnie Thomson to Davies, 2 February 1931, Blodwen Davies fonds, Vol. 11, Library and Archives Canada, MG30.

38 There are numerous anecdotes found in Littlefield, *The Thomsons of Durham*. Ajax: Durham West Arts Centre, 2005.

39 "I believe this is why Tom Thomson was such an excellent fisherman, and why he was often observed making his own lures" Dr. James MacCallum, "Tom Thomson, Painter of the North", Canadian Magazine, Mar 1918 and others.

40 Quoted from a letter from Minnie Thomson to Davies, 2 February 1931, Blodwen Davies fonds, Vol. 11, Library and Archives Canada, MG30.

41 Ibid.

42 As described in a letter from Minnie Thomson to Davies, 2 February 1931, Blodwen Davies fonds, Vol. 11, Library and Archives Canada, MG30.

43 As described in a letter from Ross to Davies, 11 June 1930, Blodwen Davies fonds, Vol. 11, Library and Archives Canada, MG30.

44 Ibid.

45 As described in a letter from Minnie Thomson to Davies, 2 February 1931, Blodwen Davies fonds, Vol. 11, Library and Archives Canada, MG30.

46 As described in an interview with Margaret Tweedale 6 September 1973, Library and Archives Canada, Harold Town fonds, Vol. 30, File 10, MG30 D404.

47 Ibid.

48 As described in a letter from Louise Thomson to Davies, 11 March 1931, Blodwen Davies fonds, Vol. 11, Library and Archives Canada, MG30.

49 Quoted from a letter from Louise Thomson to Davies, 11vMarch 1931, Blodwen Davies fonds, Vol. 11, Library and Archives Canada, MG30.

50 As described in a letter from one of Tom's sisters, whereabouts unknown.

51 As quoted from a letter from Ross to Davies, 1 June 1930, Blodwen Davies fonds, Vol. 11, Library and Archives Canada, MG30.

52 As described in a letter from Minnie Thomson to Davies, 2 February 1931, Blodwen Davies fonds, Vol. 11, Library and Archives Canada, MG30.

53 As described in Blodwen Davies, *Tom Thomson*, Mitchell Press Ltd 1967.

54 Mathew 22; 11-14.

55 Leith was established in the mid-1800s. Wikipedia contributors. "Leith, Ontario." *Wikipedia, The Free Encyclopedia.* Wikipedia, The Free Encyclopedia, 4 July 2018. Web. 12 December 2018.

56 Numerous sources, primarily Blodwen Davies, *Tom Thomson*, Mitchell, 1967.

57 As quoted from a letter by Ross to Davies, 1 June 1930, Blodwen Davies fonds, Vol. 11, Library and Archives Canada, MG30.

Chapter 3

58 As described in a letter from Minnie Thomson to Davies, 2 February 1931, Blodwen Davies fonds, Vol. 11, Library and Archives Canada, MG30.

59 As described in Town, Harold and Silcox, David P., *Tom Thomson, the Silence and the Storm*, Firefly Books, 2001.

60 A described in a letter from Ross to Davies, 11 June 1930, Blodwen Davies fonds, Vol. 11, Library and Archives Canada, MG30.

61 Ibid.

62 Ibid.

63 Quoted from a letter from Ross to Davies, 1 June 1930, Blodwen Davies fonds, Vol. 11, Library and Archives Canada, MG30.

64 Ibid.

65 As mentioned in a letter from Ross to Davies, 11 June 1930, Blodwen Davies fonds, Vol. 11, Library and Archives Canada, MG30.

66 Meservey, A. B. (2013). *Manual of Bookkeeping and Banking.* London: Forgotten Books. (Original work published 1900).

67 Quoted from a letter from Louise Thomson to Davies, 11 March 1931, Blodwen Davies fonds, Vol. 11, Library and Archives Canada, MG30.

68 Ibid.

69 Ibid.

70 Quoted from a letter from Ross to Davies, 11 June 1930, Blodwen Davies fonds, Vol. 11, Library and Archives Canada, MG30.

71 Quoted from a letter from Louise Thomson to Davies, 11 March 1931, Blodwen Davies fonds, Vol. 11, Library and Archives Canada, MG30.

72 Quoted from a letter from Fraser Thomson to Davies, 19 May 1930, Blodwen Davies fonds, Vol. 11, Library and Archives Canada, MG30.

Chapter 4

73 Quoted from a letter from Fraser Thomson to Davies, 19 May 1930, Blodwen Davies fonds, Vol. 11, Library and Archives Canada, MG30.

74 As described in Littlefield, Angie, *The Thomsons of Durham*, Envoy, 2005.

75 As described in a letter from Henry Thomson to Davies, included in letter from Ralph Thomson, 19 October 1946, Blodwen Davies fonds, Vol. 11, Library and Archives Canada, MG30.

76 Ibid.

77 Ibid.

78 As quoted in Murray, *Tom Thomson: Design for a Canadian Hero*. Dundurn, 1998.

79 As described in a letter from Henry Thomson to Davies, included in letter from Ralph Thomson, 19 October 1946, Blodwen Davies fonds, Vol. 11, Library and Archives Canada, MG30.

80 Ibid.

81 As described in King, Ross, *Defiant Spirits*, Douglas and McIntyre, 2010.

82 As quoted from Alice Lambert's novel, *Women are Like That*, Vanguard Press, 1934.

83 Ibid.

84 Sir Walter Scott, *Thomas The Rhymer.*

85 According to Alice, Rutherford told Thomson they were engaged. Another version has it that Alice giggled at Tom's proposal. Murray, Joan, Tom Thomson: *Design for a Canadian Hero.* Dundurn, 1998.

86 Ibid.

87 According to Statistics Canada, the average labourer was making 25¢ an hour, Tom was making only slightly more at about 27¢. <http://www.statcan.gc.ca/access_acces/archive.action?l=eng&loc=E248_267a-eng.csv>.

88 Littlefield, Angela. *Tom Thomson's Toronto Neighborhoods.* Toronto: Marangi Editions. 2016.

89 Quotes from a letter from Alice Lambert to Joan Murray, 1971 from Neil J. Lehto, "Alice Elinor Lambert," Algonquin Elegy, "n.d.", (12 December 2018) < http://www.algonquinelegy.com/Alice.html>.

90 Ibid.

91 As quoted in Murray, *Tom Thomson: Design for a Canadian Hero*, Dundurn 1998.

92 Ibid.

93 From the minutes of a commemorative Brodie Club meeting, William Brodie Fonds, Royal Ontario Museum Archives.

94 See Littlefield, *Tom Thomson Toronto Neighborhoods* for excellent descriptions and reimaginings of the places Thomson lived.

95 Frye, "Canadian and Colonial Painting," *The Bush Garden*, House of Anansi, 1971.

96 William Brodie, unpublished manuscript, William Brodie Fonds, Royal Ontario Museum Archive.

Chapter 5

97A As described in a letter from Minnie Thomson to Davies, 2 February 1931, Blodwen Davies fonds, Vol. 11, Library and Archives Canada, MG30.

97B From Thomas Ken, *The Doxology–Praise God, from Whom all blessings flow*, 1674.

98 Brodie, unpublished manuscript, William Brodie Fonds, Royal Ontario Museum Archive.

99 Suzanne Zeller, "BRODIE, WILLIAM," in *Dictionary of Canadian Biography*, vol. 13, University of Toronto/Université Laval, "1994", (12 December 2018). <2018, http://www.biographi.ca/en/bio/brodie_william_13E.html>.

100 From the minutes of a commemorative Brodie Club meeting, William Brodie Fonds, Royal Ontario Museum Archives.

101 Excerpt from article by Frank Barkey in *The Owen Sound Sun-Times*, 1964 quoted by Angela Littlefield "George Thomson" in *Tom Thomson*, "n.d.", (12 December 2018). <http://angielittlefield.com/TomThomson/GeorgeThomson.html>.

102 Murray, Tom Thomson, *Design for a Canadian Hero, Dundurn*, 1998.

103 Thomson's salary at Legg Brothers has been recorded at $11 a week. Perhaps that was his starting salary, and he had received a raise at that point (1907) or perhaps Minnie was mistaken. After all, the letter was written almost 25 years later. Littlefield, *Tom Thomson Toronto Neighborhoods*, Toronto: Marangi Editions. 2016.

104 As quoted from a letter from Minnie Thomson to Davies, 2 February 1931, Blodwen Davies fonds, Vol. 11, Library and Archives Canada, MG30.

105 Ibid.

106 Albert Robson, *Tom Thomson: Painter of Our North Country*, 1877-1917. Toronto: Ryerson Press, 1937.

107 Ibid.

108 As described in Ross, *Defiant Spirits*, Douglas and McIntyre, 2010.

109 Ibid.

110 Ibid.

111 This is from Stefan Zweig's description of the poet Rainer Maria Rilke, for his autobiography: *The World of Yesterday*, U of Nebraska Press, 1964, but I believe it is appropriate for MacDonald who was himself a poet.

112 As quoted in letter from Minnie Thomson to Davies, 2 February 1931, Blodwen Davies fonds, Vol. 11, Library and Archives Canada, MG30-D24.

113 Littlefield, *Tom Thomson's Toronto Neighborhoods*, Toronto: Marangi Editions. 2016.

114 This story appears in Ottelyn Addison, *Tom Thomson, the Algonquin Years*, McGraw-Hill Ryerson, 1995.

115 Ibid.

116 As described in Davies, *Tom Thomson*, Mitchell Press, 1967.

117 Sir Walter Scott, *Thomas The Rhymer.*

118 As described in Davies, *Tom Thomson,* Mitchell Press, 1967.

119 The motto of the Toronto Art Students' League. <http://www.thecanadianencyclopedia.ca/en/article/drawing/>.

120 Davies, *Tom Thomson,* Mitchell Press, 1967.

121 As described in a letter from HB Jackson to Davies, 5 May 1931, Blodwen Davies fonds, Vol. 11, Library and Archives Canada, MG30-D24.

122 Edgar Allan Poe, *Eulalie,* from <http://www.poemhunter.com/poem/eulalie/>. Eulalie was the name of Tom's dog. How long he had that dog, or why she was called Eulalie is unknown. In fact, the only mention of the dog I have found is the photograph pictured.

123 Quoted from a letter from HB Jackson to Davies, 5 May 1931, Blodwen Davies fonds, Vol. 11, Library and Archives Canada, MG30-D24.

124 As described in a letter from one of Tom's sisters, whereabouts unknown.

125 Ross King, *Defiant Spirits,* Douglas and McIntyre, 2010 and Kevin Plumber, "Forgotten Urban Squalor of The Ward," in *The Torontoist,* 11 October 2008. <http://torontoist.com/2008/10/historicist_forgotten_urban_squalor_1/>.

126 Although Tom was not a member, he would have attended shows there, so why not lunch?

127 As described by A.Y. Jackson in Wayne Larsen, A.Y. Jackson: *The Life of a Landscape Painter,* Dundurn Press, 2009.

128 Littlefield, *Tom Thomson Toronto Neighborhoods,* Marangi Editions, 2010.

129 MacGregor, Roy, *Northern Light,* Vintage Canada, 2010.

130 As described in a letter from HB Jackson to Davies, 5 May 1931, Blodwen Davies fonds, Vol. 11, Library and Archives Canada, MG30-D24.

131 Mark Robinson quoted from *Mark Robinson in conversation with J. Alex Edmison*, p.1. Tom Thomson Collection, McMichael Canadian Art Collection Archives, 1953.

132 Ibid.

133 Ibid.

134 Ibid.

135 Quoted from a letter from Harry Jackson to Davies, 29 April 1931, Blodwen Davies fonds, Vol. 11, Library and Archives Canada, MG30-D24.

136 "While we were together he did very little serious sketching, making a few notes, sky lines & color effects." HB Jackson letter to Davies, 5 May 1931, Blodwen Davies fonds, Vol. 11, Library and Archives Canada, MG30-D24.

Chapter 6

137 Quoted from a letter from Harry Jackson to Davies, 5 May 1931, Blodwen Davies fonds, Vol. 11, Library and Archives Canada, MG30-D24.

138 Walton, Izaak, *The Compleat Angler.*

139 Quoted from a letter from Harry Jackson to Blodwen Davies, 5 May 1931, Blodwen Davies fonds, Vol. 11, Library and Archives Canada, MG30-D24.

140 Quoted by Mark Robinson in taped recollections of Mark Robinson in conversation with J. Alex Edmison in Tom Thomson Collection, McMichael Canadian Art Collection Archives. Guide Ralph Bice is also quoted as saying

Thomson, "was not very proficient in a canoe." MacGregor, Roy, *Northern Light*, Vintage Canada, 2010.

141 Quoted by Mark Robinson in taped recollections of Mark Robinson in conversation with J. Alex Edmison in Tom Thomson Collection, McMichael Canadian Art Collection Archives.

142 119 Summerhill Ave. according to Tippet, Maria, *Stormy Weather, FH Varley, A Biography*, McClelland and Stewart, 1998.

143 As quoted in Tippett, Maria, Stormy Weather: F.H. Varley a Biography, McClelland and Stewart Inc., 1998.

144 King, *Defiant Spirits*, Douglas and McIntyre, 2010.

145 Ibid.

146 "Local Man's Experience in Northern Wilds," *The Owen Sound Sun*, 27 September 1912.

147 As described in Tom Thomson's letter to Dr. M.J. McRuer, 17 October 1912, McMichael Canadian Art Collection Archives.

148 Quoted in a letter from Louise Thomson to Davies, 1931, Blodwen Davies fonds, Vol. 11, Library and Archives Canada, MG30-D24.

149 Ibid.

150 Arthur Lismer as quoted in McLeish, *September Gale, A Life of Arthur Lismer*, Dent, 1973.

151 Robson, *Tom Thomson, Painter of our North Country*, Ryerson 1951.

152 Ibid.

153 MacCallum, "Tom Thomson, Painter of the North," The Canadian Magazine, March 1918.

154 As quoted in Davies, Blodwen, *Paddle and Palette: (The Story of Tom Thomson)*, Ryerson, 1930.

155 Burns, Robert, *The Selkirk Grace.*

156 Robson, *Tom Thomson, Painter of our North Country*, Ryerson, 1951.

157 As described in Murray, *Tom Thomson: Design for a Canadian Hero*, Dundurn, 1998.

158 Kyle, Fergus, "The Ontario Society of Artists," In The Year Book of Canadian Art 1913. <https://archive.org/stream/1912bookofcanadi00artsuoft/1912bookofcanadi00artsuoft_djvu.txt>.

159 Burns, Robert, *The Selkirk Grace.*

160 Maud Varley quoted in Tippett, *Stormy Weather, F.H. Varley a Biography*, McClelland and Stewart, 1998.

161 Fred Varley quoted in Tippett, *Stormy Weather, F.H. Varley a Biography*, McClelland and Stewart, 1998.

162 As described in Tippett, *Stormy Weather, F.H. Varley a Biography*, McClelland and Stewart, 1998.

163 Quoted in Davies, *Tom Thomson*, Mitchell Press Limited, 1967.

164 King, *Defiant Spirits*, Douglas and McIntyre, 2010.

165 Thoreau MacDonald relating his father J.E.H.'s memories in "Recollections of Thoreau MacDonald," In Addison, *Tom Thomson: The Algonquin Years*, McGraw-Hill, 1995.

166 As described by Dr. R. P. Little "Some Recollections of Tom Thomson and Canoe Lake," Culture, 1955. <http://www.canadianmysteries.ca/sites/thomson/archives/journalarticle/5256en.html>.

167 Quoted by Roy MacGregor in *Northern Light*, Vintage Canada 2010.

168 Ibid.

169 Quoted by Mark Robinson in taped recollections of Mark Robinson in conversation with J. Alex Edmison in Tom Thomson Collection, McMichael Canadian Art Collection Archives.

170 Ibid.

171 MacCallum, J.M., "Tom Thomson, Painter of the North," *The Canadian Magazine*, March 1918.

172 Quoted from a letter by A.Y. Jackson to Lawren Harris, 26 March 1913, Library and Archives Canada, Naomi Jackson Groves fonds, MG30-D351.

173 As described in A.Y. Jackson letter to Lawren Harris, 26 March 1913 Library and Archives Canada, Naomi Jackson Groves fonds, MG30-D351.

174 A.Y. Jackson quoted in "Foreword of Catalog of an Exhibition by the Late Tom Thomson," *The Montreal Arts Club*, March 1-21, 1919.

175 As described in AY Jackson's Forward to Davies, *Tom Thomson*, Mitchell, 1967.

176 Littlefield, *Tom Thomson's Toronto Neighborhoods*, Marangi Editions, 2016.

177 Franklin Carmichael as quoted in Davies, *Tom Thomson*, Mitchell, 1967.

178 A Recollection of Tom Thomson by S.H.F. Kemp in Little, *The Tom Thomson Mystery*, McGraw-Hill Ryerson, 1970.

179 Recollections of Thoreau MacDonald in Addison, *Tom Thomson: The Algonquin Years*, McGraw-Hill, 1995.

180 King, *Defiant Spirits*, Douglas and McIntyre, 2010.

181 Gadsby, Henry, "Peter and I," *Toronto Daily Star*, 12 December 1913.

182 MacDonald, J.E.H, *Toronto Daily Star*, 18 December 1913.

183 Augustus Brindle, arts journalist and founder of the Arts and Letters Club. "Beatty, according to Brindle, was a "glorious truculent bigot." *Arts & Letters Club newsletter* 1982.

185 King, *Defiant Spirits*, Douglas and McIntyre, 2010.

186 Quotes from a letter from Tom Thomson to J.E.H. MacDonald, 22 July 1915 "As with yourself I can't get used to the idea of Jackson being in the machine and it is rotten that in this so called civilized age that such things can exist but since this war has started it will have to go on until our side wins out." Archives of Ontario, William Colgate Collection, MU583/F1066.

Chapter 7

187 Mark Robinson attributed this phrase to Thomson as described it Murray, *Tom Thomson, The Last Spring*, Dundurn, 1994.

188 Quoted from a letter by Franklin Carmichael to his fiancé, Ada Went, McMichael Art Gallery Archives.

189 As described in Larisey, *Light for a Cold Land: Lawren Harris's Life and Work*, Dundurn, 1993.

190 King, *Defiant Spirits*, Douglas and McIntyre, 2010.

191 As described in Davies, *Tom Thomson*, Mitchell, 1967.

192 Quoted from a letter from AY Jackson to J.E.H. MacDonald, 14 February 1914, J.E.H. MacDonald Fonds, National Archives of Canada.

193 Ibid.

194 From Algonquin Park ranger Bud Callighen's journal, Archives of Ontario.

195 Quoted in Murray, *Tom Thomson: Design for a Canadian Hero*, Dundurn, 1998.

196 McCallum, "Tom Thomson: Painter of the North," *The Canadian Magazine*, Mar 1918.

197 As described in King, *Defiant Spirits*, Douglas and McIntyre, 2010.

198 Quoted from Tom Thomson letter to Fred Varley, 8 July 1914, The Tom Thomson Collection, McMichael Canadian Art Collection Archives.

199 Quoted by Mark Robinson in taped recollections of Mark Robinson in conversation with J. Alex Edmison in Tom Thomson Collection, McMichael Canadian Art Collection Archives.

200 Quoted from Tom Thomson letter to Fred Varley, 8 July 1914, The Tom Thomson Collection, McMichael Canadian Art Collection Archives.

201 From Algonquin Park ranger Bud Callighen's journal, Archives of Ontario.

202 Quoted from letter in Larsen, AY Jackson: *Life of a Landscape Painter*, Dundurn, 2009.

203 Jackson, A.Y. *A Painter's Country*, Toronto, Clarke Irwin 1958.

204 Quoted from A.Y. Jackson letter to J.E.H. MacDonald, 5 October 1914, Library and Archives Canada.

205 Quoted from Davies, *Tom Thomson*, Mitchell Press, 1967.

206 Quoted from letter by Tom Thomson to Dr. MacCallum 6 October 1914, Library and Archives, National Gallery of Canada, Dr. James M. McCallum Papers.

207 Quoted from Tippet, *Stormy Weather*, McClelland & Stewart, 2000.

208 Jackson, *A Painter's Country*, Toronto, Clarke, Irwin, 1958.

209 Quoted from Jackson, A.Y., *A Painter's Country*, Clarke, Irwin, 1967.

210 Quoted from a letter by Franklin Carmichael to his fiancé Ada Went, 6 February 1914, McMichael Archives.

211 Quoted from a letter by Franklin Carmichael to Ada Went, 1 February 1915, McMichael Archives.

212 Quoted from a letter by Franklin Carmichael to Ada Went, 6 February 1914, McMichael Archives.

213 Ibid.

214 Ibid.

215 *Toronto Star*, 26 November 1914.

216 *Mail and Empire*, 13 March 1915.

217 From Lawren Harris's unpublished poem, Old Pine in personal journal, Library and Archives Canada.

218 From ranger Bud Callighen's journal, 28 April 1915, Archives of Ontario.

219 Quoted from letter by Franklin Carmichael to Ada Went, 25 May 1915, McMichael Archives.

220 Quoted from a letter by Tom Thomson to J.E.H. MacDonald, 22 July 1915, Archives of Ontario, William Colgate Collection, MU583/F1066.

221 Quoted from Jackson, *A Painter's Country: the autobiography of AY Jackson*, Clarke, Irwin, 1967.

222 Quoted from a letter by Tom Thomson to J.E.H. MacDonald, 22 July 1915, Archives of Ontario, William Colgate Collection, MU583/F1066.

223 From the Anglican funeral service <https://churchofengland.org/prayer-worship/worship/texts/pastoral/funeral/funeral.aspx>.

224 1 Timothy 6.7; Job 1.21b.

225 King, *Defiant Spirits*, Douglas and McIntyre, 2010.

226 Written on the back of Tom Thomson sketch, *Sand Hill* by Dr. James MacCallum, Art Gallery of Ontario.

227 As described by T.W. Kidd in Addison, *Tom Thomson The Algonquin Years*, McGraw-Hill Ryerson, 1995.

228 Quoted by Mark Robinson in taped recollections of Mark Robinson in conversation with J. Alex Edmison in Tom Thomson Collection, McMichael Canadian Art Collection Archives.

229 Ibid.

230 As described in Minnie Thomson letter to Davies, 2 February 1931 and by Bud Callighen in Little, "Some Recollections of Tom Thomson and Canoe Lake," *Culture*, 1955. Tom's friend and coworker Stanley Kemp has argued that Thomson was a pacifist and would never have enlisted.

231 As recorded in Addison, *Tom Thomson the Algonquin Years*, McGraw-Hill Ryerson, 1995.

232 Quoted from a letter by Franklin Carmichael to Ada Went, 15 May 1915, McMichael Archives.

233 Quoted from a letter by Tom Thomson to Dr. MacCallum, 9 September 1915, Library and Archives, National Gallery of Canada, Dr. James M. McCallum Papers.

234 As described in King, *Defiant Spirits*, Douglas and McIntyre, 2010.

235 Quoted from a letter by Minnie Thomson to Davies, 2 February 1931, Blodwen Davies fonds, Vol. 11, Library and Archives Canada, MG30-D24.

236 As per Murray, *A Treasury of Tom Thomson*, Douglas and McIntyre, 2011.

237 Ibid.

238 As described in interview with Mark Robinson by Alex Edmison, Date 1952, Library and Archives, National Gallery of Canada.

239 Quoted from a letter by Tom Thomson to John Thomson, 16 April 1917, Library and Archives Canada, Tom Thomson Collection, MG30 D284.

240 As described in Murray, *Tom Thomson: Design for a Canadian Hero*, Dundurn, 1998.

241 Ibid.

Chapter 8

242 "Reminiscences by Thoreau MacDonald," In Addison, *Tom Thomson, the Algonquin Years*, McGraw-Hill Ryerson, 1995.

243 Jim Buris, Lyrics, Chris Smith, Music, *Ballin' the Jack*, Jos. W. Stern & Co. 1913.

244 Quoted from the journal of M.O. Hammond, MO Hammond Fonds, Archives of Ontario.

245 Ibid.

246 Estelle M. Kerr, *The Courier*, 25 March 1916.

247 T. Pritchard, Lyrics, Jules Brazil, Music, *The Call*, in "Boys of Canada": *Songs from the First World War*, Independent Publishing Co., 1914-1918.

248 Quoted from "Some Pictures at the Art Gallery" *Toronto Daily Star*, 11 March 1916.

249 Quoted from "Pictures That Can be Heard" *Saturday Night Magazine*, 8 March 1916.

250 Ibid.

251 Ibid.

252 Ibid.

253 Ibid.

254 Quoted from letter by J.E.H. MacDonald in *The Globe*, 15 March 1916.

255 Painter and Art Critic Carl Ahrens interviewed in *The Toronto Daily Star*, 16 March 1916.

256 Lawren S. Harris, *The Story of the Group of Seven*, Rous and Mann Press, 1964.

257 Shelley, Percy Bysshe, *Ode To The West Wind.*

258 Telegram to Mrs. Jackson, 11 June 1916, location unknown.

259 Quoted from a letter from Tom Thomson to Dr. MacCallum, 4 October 1916, Library and Archives, National Gallery of Canada, Dr. James M. MacCallum Papers.

260 Murray, *Tom Thomson Catalogue Raisonne*, < http://tomthomsoncatalogue.org>.

261 Compare Lismer's *September Gale*, *Carmichael's Island Georgian Bay* and Varley's *Stormy Weather* all painted after Thomson's *West Wind.*

262 "Reminiscences by Thoreau MacDonald," In Addison, *Tom Thomson, the Algonquin Years*, McGraw-Hill Ryerson, 1995.

263 Quoted from interview with Mark Robinson by Alex Edmison, Date 1952, Library and Archives, National Gallery of Canada.

264 Quoted from letter by James McCallum to Bobby, 29 April 1931, Archives of Ontario, William Colgate Collection, MU583/F1066.

265 Quoted from Interview with Daphne Crombie by Ronald Pittaway, 14 January 1977, Algonquin Park Museum Archives.

266 Ibid.

267 Ibid.

268 *The Owen Sound Sun*, April 10, 1917.

269 Quoted from a letter by Tom Thomson to Tom Harkness, 31 April 1917, Library and Archives Canada, Tom Thomson Collection, MG30 D284.

270 Quoted from interview with Mark Robinson by Alex Edmison, Date 1952, Library and Archives, National Gallery of Canada.

271 As described in Addison, *Tom Thomson, the Algonquin Years*, McGraw-Hill Ryerson, 1995.

272 Quoted from a letter by Doctor James MacCallum to Tom Thomson, 28 May 1917, Library and Archives Canada, Tom Thomson Collection, MG30 D284.

273 Quoted from interview with Mark Robinson by Alex Edmison, Date 1952, Library and Archives, National Gallery of Canada.

274 Quoted from a letter from Mark Robinson to Blodwen Davies, 23 March 1930, Blodwen Davies fonds, Vol. 11, Library and Archives Canada, MG30-D24.

275 Quoted from a letter from Tom Thomson to James MacCallum, 7 July 1917, Library and Archives, National Gallery of Canada, Dr. James M. MacCallum Papers.

276 Quoted from a letter from Mark Robinson to Blodwen Davies, 23 March 1930, Blodwen Davies fonds, Vol. 11, Library and Archives Canada, MG30-D24.

277 Quoted from "Application for the exhumation of the body of one Thos. Thomson drowned in Canoe Lake in 1917" by Blodwen Davies, 27 July1931, Archives of Ontario.

278 *Thomas the Rhymer*, Sir Walter Scott.

279 Quotes from a letter by A.Y. Jackson to J.E.H. MacDonald, 26 August 1917, Library and Archives Canada.

280 Quoted from a letter from Margaret Thomson to Dr. James MacCallum, 2 August 1917, Archives of Ontario, William Colgate Collection, MU583/F1066.

281 P.G. Konody "The palace of arts at Wembley," In *The Observer*, London, 24 May 1925.

282 "It was Tom I had in mind—his remoteness, his genius, his reticence." Lawren Harris in regard to his painting *A Memorium to a Canadian Artist*, 1950 as contained in Murray, *Canadian Art in the Twentieth Century*, Dundurn, 1999.

283 "Tom Thomson still stands as the Canadian painter, harsh, brilliant, brittle, uncouth, not only the most Canadian but most creative." David Milne in Milne Family Papers, December 1930.

284 W.H. Auden, *In Memory of W.B. Yeats*.

Bibliography

I cannot thank enough, the writers of these titles from which I drew so much inspiration and information, for this book. These are the giants on whose shoulders I am attempting to stand.

Davies, Blodwen, *Paddle and Palette.* Toronto: Ryerson Press, 1930.

Davies, Blodwen, *Tom Thomson.* Vancouver: Mitchell Press Limited, 1967.

Blodwen Davies fonds, Vol. 11. Library and Archives Canada, MG30 D38, February 2, 1931.

Davies was Thomson's first biographer, and she exchanged letters with many of Tom's friends and family. These letters are now housed in Library and Archives Canada. All subsequent writers have drawn upon her work.

Silcox, David and Town, Harold. *Tom Thomson: The Silence and The Storm.* Willowdale: Firefly Books, 2001.

Originally released in 1977, this was the first large-format book to showcase Tom's art and turned many of my generation on to Thomson's art. There's lots of zesty, and occasionally inappropriate, commentary from Town.

Murray, Joan. *Tom Thomson, Design for a Canadian Hero.* Toronto: Dundurn Press, 1998.

Murray, Joan. *Tom Thomson, The Last Spring.* Toronto: Dundurn Press, 1994.

Murray, Joan. *A Treasury of Tom Thomson.* Vancouver: Douglas & McIntyre, 2011.

Murray, Joan. *Canadian Art in the Twentieth Century.* Toronto: Dundurn Press, 1999.

The undisputed expert on all things Thomson, Murray has also generously contributed much of her correspondence and research to Library and Archives Canada. Murray was the first biographer to grasp the importance of William Brodie to Tom's art.

King, Ross. *Defiant Spirits: The Modernist Revolution of The Group Of Seven.* Toronto: Douglas & McIntyre, 2010.

Tremendously well-researched and documented, this book is a must-have for any fan of Thomson and/or The Group of Seven. The wartime episodes in my book owe much to Mr. King'.

MacGregor, Roy. *Northern Light: The Enduring Mystery of Tom Thomson and The Woman Who Loved Him.* Toronto: Random House Canada, 2010.

Mr. MacGregor solves the mystery of Tom's burial place and presents a compelling argument as to the manner of Thomson's death and the exact nature of his relationship with Winnie Trainor.

Littlefield, Angela. *The Thomsons of Durham.* Ajax: Durham West Arts Centre, 2005.

Littlefield, Angela. *Tom Thomson's Toronto Neighborhoods.* Toronto: Marangi Editions, 2016.

Littlefield, Angela. *Tom Thomson.* "n.d." (12 December 2018). < http://angielittlefield.com/TomThomson.html>

The Claremont and Toronto chapters of my book owe much to Littlefield's evocative imaginings and diligent research.

Grace, Sherill. *Inventing Tom Thomson.* Montreal: McGill-Queen's University Press, 2004.

Grace's in-depth analysis of the many depictions of Thomson and insightful commentary create a nuanced picture of the artist that I found tremendously useful.

Three websites that I found extremely useful, and returned to repeatedly:

Hozer, Michèle and Raymont, Peter. *West Wind, the vision of Tom Thomson,* White Pine Pictures, 2011. <tomthomsonart.com>.

Klages, Gregory. "Death on a Painted Lake: The Tom Thomson Tragedy" 2008. <canadianmysteries.ca/sites/thomson/indexen.html>.

Murray, Joan. *Tom Thomson, Catalogue Raisonné.* 2018. (12 December 2018) < http://tomthomsoncatalogue.org>.

Other Important Sources

Addison, Ottelyn. *Tom Thomson: The Algonquin Years.* Toronto: Ryerson Press, 1969.

Arthur Lismer and Marjorie Lismer Bridges Fonds, Edward P. Taylor Research Library and Archives, Art Gallery of Ontario.

William Brodie fonds, Royal Ontario Museum Archives.

Dr. James M. McCallum Papers, Library and Archives, National Gallery of Canada.

Edmison, Alex. *Mark Robinson in conversation with J. Alex Edmison, p.1.* Tom Thomson Collection, McMichael Canadian Art Collection Archives, 1953.

Frye, Northrop. *The Bush Garden.* House of Anansi, 1971.

Gauslin, Lilian. *From Paths to Planes. Story of the Claremont Area.* Claremont, Self Published, 1974.

Harris, Lawren S. *The Story of the Group of Seven.* Toronto: Rous and Mann Press, 1964.

Hubbard, R.H. *Tom Thomson.* Toronto: Society for Art Publications, 1962.

Hunter, Andrew. *Up North: A Northern Ontario Tragedy.* Owen Sound: Tom Thomson Books, 1997.

Jackson, A.Y. *A Painter's Country.* Toronto: Clarke Irwin, 1958.

King James Bible. *Bible Hub.* n.d. (12 December 2018). < https://biblehub.com/kjv/genesis/1.htm>.

Larisey, Peter. *Light for a Cold Land: Lawren Harris's Life and Work.* Toronto: Dundurn, 1993.

Larsen, Wayne. *Tom Thomson: Artist of the North.* Toronto: Dundurn Press, 2011.

Larsen, Wayne. *A.Y. Jackson: The Life of a Landscape Painter.* Toronto: Dundurn Press, 2009.

Lehto, Neil, J. *Algonquin Elegy.* Bloomington: iUniverse, Inc, 2005.

Little, William T. *The Tom Thomson Mystery.* Toronto: McGraw-Hill, 1970.

MacCallum, James. "Tom Thomson, Painter of the North", *Canadian Magazine.* Mar 1918.

McLeish, John A.B. *September Gale, A Life of Arthur Lismer.* Toronto: Dent, 1973.

Newlands, Anne. *The Group of Seven and Tom Thomson, An Introduction.* Willowdale: Firefly Books, 1995.

Ontario Ministry of Transportation. n.d. (12 December 2018). < http://www.mto.gov.on.ca/english/traveller/map/northindexpdf.shtml>.

Plumber, Kevin. "Forgotten Urban Squalor of The Ward," in *The Torontoist.* 11 October 2008. <http://torontoist.com/2008/10/historicist_forgotten_urban_squalor_1/>.

Reid, Dennis ed. *Tom Thomson.* Vancouver: D&M Publishers, 2010.

Robson, Albert Henry. *Tom Thomson.* Toronto: Ryerson Press, 1937.

Robson, Albert. *Tom Thomson: Painter of Our North Country, 1877-1917.* Toronto: Ryerson Press, 1937.

Shaw, Bernard S. Canoe Lake, *Algonquin Park: Tom Thomson and Other Mysteries.* Burnstown: General Store, 1996.

Tippett, Maria. *Stormy Weather: F.H. Varley, A Biography.* Toronto: M&S, 1998.

Tom Thomson Collection, Library and Archives Canada.

Wikipedia contributors. "Algonquin Provincial Park". In *Wikipedia, The Free Encyclopedia.* 16 November 2018. (12 December 2018). < https://en.wikipedia.org/wiki/Algonquin_Provincial_Park>.

Wikipedia contributors. "Leith, Ontario" In *Wikipedia, The Free Encyclopedia.* 4 July 2018 (12 December 2018). <https://en.wikipedia.org/wiki/Leith,_Ontario>.

Wood, William, W. *Past Years in Pickering: Sketches of the History of the Community.* 1911. (12 December 2018). <http:/www.archive.org/stream/pastyearsinpicke00wooduoft>.

Zeller, Suzanne. *"William Brodie Biography," Dictionary of Canadian Biography.* 1994. (12 December 2018). <http://www.biographi.ca/en/bio/brodie_william_13E.html>.

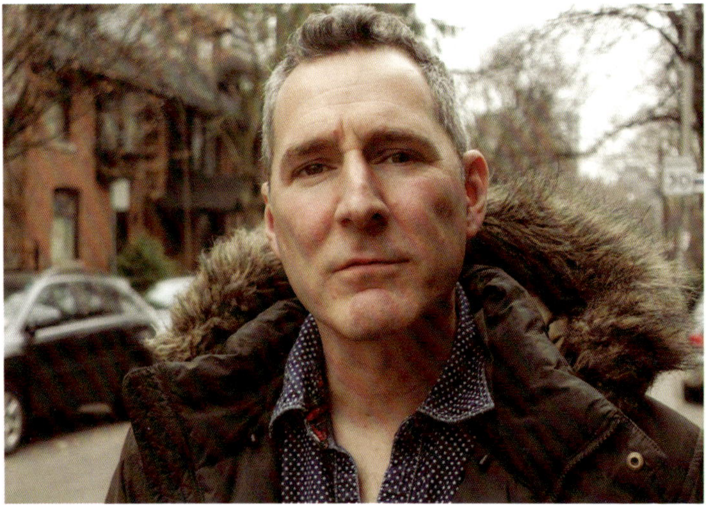

Author photo by Jack Neary

Richard Weiser

Richard Weiser is a writer of prose, poetry, song lyrics and ad copy. He began his working life in broadcast journalism after which he returned to school to study creative writing with Governor General's Award winner Don Coles. After university, Richard tripped and fell into a career in advertising and recently won a Cannes Lion (advertising's version of the Oscar).

Richard worked on his Tom Thomson manuscript with Olive Senior at the Humber School for Writers in 2014. He is a member of the League of Canadian Poets and SOCAN and his poetry has been published internationally in journals such as HCE, Acumen and Gravel. Richard lives in Toronto with his partner and two children.